A Place in the Sun

Dream Homes Within Your Reach

Fanny Blake

with an introduction by
Amanda Lamb

First published in 2003 by Channel 4 Books,
an imprint of Pan Macmillan Ltd,
Pan Macmillan, 20 New Wharf Road, London N1 9RR,
Basingstoke and Oxford.

Associated companies throughout the world

www.panmacmillan.com

ISBN 0 7522 1588 4

Introduction © Amanda Lamb 2003
Text © Fanny Blake, 2003

Design by Perfect Bound Ltd
Colour reproduction by Aylesbury Studios Ltd
Printed and bound in Great Britain by Butler and Tanner

The information given in the climate charts is taken from
www.weatherbase.com.

This book accompanies the television series *A Place in the Sun*
made by Freeform Productions for Channel 4.
Executive producers: Ann Lavelle and Antoine Palmer

Picture Credits

Contents page 3: beaches shot (see also p6) – *The Travel Library*;
countryside shot (see also p50) – *The Travel Library*; mountains shot
(see also p96) – *World Pictures*, islands shot (see also p134) –
The Travel Library; p6 – *The Travel Library*; p8,10,11 – *Corbis*;
p14 – Cindy Van Hoof; p15, 17, 18 – *Corbis*; p19 top – Keith and
Elaine Short; p21 – Tony and Carol Tidswell; p22 – *PictureBank Photo
Library Ltd*; p24 – *Corbis*; p25, 26 top – Adrian and Patricia Taylor; p28
– Lynne and Neville Stock; p29, 31 – *World Pictures*;
p32 – *Corbis*; p33 top – Mark and Ali Lodge; p35 – Angus Kirk;
p37 – *Corbis*; p39, 40 – *Corbis*; p41 top – Eamon and Claire Belton;
p43 – Peter and Jacqui Wright; p44 – *Travel Ink/David Martyn Hughes*;
p46, 47 – *Corbis*; p48 top – Pauline Andrew and Joe McKenna; p50,
52 – *World Pictures*; p53 – *The Travel Library*;
p54 top – Matt Lewis and Nikki Bates; p56 – Gerry and Linda Jack;
p58 – *The Travel Library*; p60 – *Corbis*; p62 – *Travel Ink/Jill Swainson*;
p63 – *Corbis*; p66 – Steve and Sylvia Sales; p67 – *World Pictures*; p69,
70 – *Corbis*; p71 top – Peter and Denise Scott;
p73 – Ian Thomas; p74, 76, 77 – *Corbis*; p78 top – Gilbert Crabtree
and Janet Townley; p80 – Matt and Alison Howard; p81, 83, 84 – *The
Travel Library*; p87 – Philippa Sharman; p88 – *World Pictures*;
p90, 91 – *The Travel Library*; p92 top – Dave and Wendy Southwell;
p94 – Susan Guillerand; p96 – *World Pictures*; p98 – *The Travel
Library*; p100 – Granada Properties, Andalucia; p101 – *The Travel
Library*; p104 – Clare Sasada; p105, 106 – *Corbis*; p107 – Gilly de
Conti; p109 top – David Exley and Anita Cutts; p111 – Gilly de Conti;
p112 – *The Travel Library*; p114, 115 – *Corbis*; p116 top – John and
Margaret Harpin; p118 – Eileen and Geoffrey Brown; p119, 121 – *The
Travel Library*; p122 – *Corbis*; p123 top – Jean Bentley;
p125 – Clive Jarman; p126 – *World Pictures*; p128, 129 – *Corbis*;
p130 top – Barry and Liz Crane; p132 – Ben and Sammi Pease;
p134, 136 – *The Travel Library*; p138 – *World Pictures*; p139 –
The Travel Library; p140 top – David and Fiona Bolton; p143, 145 –
The Travel Library; p146 – *World Pictures*; p147 top – Johnny and
Yvette Rice; p149 – Anna Asvestas; p150 – *The Travel Library*;
p152 – *World Pictures*; p153 – *Travel Ink/Abbie Enock*; p156 –
Kenneth and Sallie Wakeham. All other pictures – Channel 4.
Maps derived from Mountain High Maps © copyright 1995 Digital
Wisdom, Inc.

Notes

The prices given for properties visited by house-hunters are accurate
for the exchange rate at the time of the visit.

Measurements

Foreign property is measured metrically. One hectare (10,000 square
metres) equals 2.471 acres (12,000 square yards). One acre (4840
square yards) equals approximately 4,050 square metres.

Thanks

The author would like to thank Alasdair Riley
who helped research the book.

Contents

Introduction

by Amanda Lamb

Hello and thank you for buying *A Place in the Sun: Dream Homes Within Your Reach*. I hope you enjoy reading it and, more importantly, that you find it useful if you are thinking of buying your own place in the sun. It's packed full of important information, stunning and evocative photographs and, of course, interviews with people who are looking to take the plunge, as well as those who have already bought their dream home abroad.

It's been three years now since I first began filming for *A Place in the Sun*, a fact I still find hard to believe, as it seems like only yesterday. During that time we have travelled all over the world in a bid to find people their very own piece of paradise. We have helped so many people find an amazing variety of properties, from ancient apartments built into city walls, to ultramodern houses ten minutes from the beach. Ramshackle barns only the most determined of house-hunters would take on, to interior-designed showhouses, where the only thing they needed to change is into their bikinis!

One of the fundamental things I have learned since presenting the programme is that everybody has a different idea of what and where their dream home would be. Not everyone's idea of heaven is a house on the beach. Some would much rather be relaxing with a glass of wine, watching the sunset, high up in a mountain village, miles away from civilization. Other people's idea of utopia is a place in the middle of the country, with only a few goats for company. Which is why we have decided to split this book into themes. The themes we have chosen are Beaches, Mountains, Islands and the Countryside. For each section, we will be looking at several areas around Europe and the Canary Islands that we believe epitomise these perfectly.

Another aim of the book is to concentrate on destinations that are increasingly both easy and feasible to get to and live in. I have lost count of the number of times I have been stuck in traffic on the M25 or squashed in the carriage of a train that hasn't moved for 30 minutes and fumed to myself, 'I could get to Spain or France quicker than it is taking me to get home!' Sound familiar? Well, for this book we are focusing mostly on destinations that the budget airlines fly to, so they are quick and cheap to visit again and again and you won't have to travel too far once you arrive at the airport.

One note of caution, however, is to remember that this book is only meant as a general guide to buying abroad and is not a substitute for the professional advice you should seek if you are thinking of buying a particular property abroad.

Feeling inspired? I hope so. The rewards of owning your very own place in the sun can be immense. Out of all the people I have met who have made the move, not one of them has regretted it. In fact, one house-hunter even went as far as to say that moving to Spain has given him a new lease of life!

I wish you the very best of luck in following your dreams.

Happy house-hunting,
Amanda Lamb

Beaches

'I see the children sport upon the shore,
And hear the mighty waters rolling evermore.'
**William Wordsworth,
'Ode. Intimations of Immortality', 1807**

The Spanish Algarve

Andalucia, Spain

The Spanish Algarve is not a name found on a map of Spain, but it is increasingly appearing in brochures to describe the coast from the Portuguese border eastwards to the Spanish city of Huelva, and sometimes even further along the Costa de la Luz towards Cádiz. Its coastline is longer than its Portuguese rival but attracts only half the number of European visitors, so its beaches, pine-strewn dunes and lagoons remain some of the least discovered in Europe. The opening of the Guadiana Bridge in 1961 brought more traffic from Portugal, but made Faro the nearest convenient airport.

The region has a long history dominated by the struggles between the Moors and Christians. The coastline has played its part, whether as a frontier against raiders (hence so many towns near Cádiz adding 'de la Frontera' to their name), as a starting point for the exploratory voyages of Columbus and Magellan, or as a link with the Napoleonic Wars, particularly the Battle of Trafalgar. Bronze Age cave dwellings, Roman remains and ruined Moorish fortresses all attest to the area's diverse past.

Andalucían traditions are alive and well here. Fiestas abound, including the Cádiz carnival (February/March), the Jerez grape harvest festival (September), El Rocío (May/June) pilgrimage to the Virgen el Rocío and the Jerez horse fair (May). Traditional cuisine is simple, often fish based. *Choco* (large squid) is a speciality, as is Jabugo ham.

highlights

❊ Tour of a sherry *bodega* in Jerez de la Frontera
❊ Watching wildlife in the Parque Nacional de Doñana
❊ La Rábida, Palos de la Frontera, Moguer – the towns connected with Columbus's expeditions
❊ Romería del Rocío – Pentecost celebration that attracts thousands of participants from all over Spain
❊ Cádiz Cathedral

Where to go

The stretch of coast from the River Guadiana, the border with Portugal, to Huelva is largely undeveloped with four protected nature reserves. The resorts are relatively modest affairs, notably **Ayamonte** and **Isla Cristina**. Ayamonte is an old fishing town, its streets and squares lined with craft shops, restaurants and bars as they descend to the working harbour. Isla Cristina, once an island, is still an important fishing port although tourism is on the rise. Nearby **Isla Canela** is by far the most developed, with 3,000 apartments already built and plenty of ongoing construction, and a growing reputation as a glitzy resort.

The major town of Huelva province is **Huelva** itself. Largely destroyed by the 1755 earthquake that decimated Lisbon, it has little of historic interest, its real attractions lying in the country and coast around it. To the south lie more expanses of sandy beach and the major resorts of **Mazagón** and **Matalascañas** next to the Parque Nacional Doñana, a wetland habitat attracting hundreds of different species of birds and other wildlife. Inland from Huelva, traditional Andalucía is to be found with numerous whitewashed villages and stud farms where the internationally renowned horses are bred. Furthest north is the Sierra de Aracena dotted with the remains of Moorish fortresses, as well as attractive villages such as **Alájar** beneath the sanctuary of Nuestra Señora de los Angeles, **Jabugo**, famed for its superb *jamón serrano* (smoked ham), and the beautifully situated **Zufre**.

Further south lies the coastline of Cádiz province. The significance of **Cádiz** itself is as a sea port, but the city is one of Europe's oldest. The town reached its heyday during the eighteenth century so beside the lively narrow streets of the old town are open squares edged by fine eighteenth-century houses. Cádiz province has over thirty miles of coastline ranging from long stretches of sandy beaches to secluded coves. The authorities have seen what has happened on the Costa del Sol and have strict building regulations in place to preserve the landscape. The resorts of **El Puerto de Santa María**, **Rota**, **Chipiona** and **Sanlúcar de Barrameda** are frequented by Spanish holidaymakers and front vast golden sands. The province is best known for breeding the *toros bravos*, the Spanish fighting bulls that are one of Andalucía's emblems. But, as importantly, it is known for its sherry production, centred on the town of **Jerez de la Frontera**.

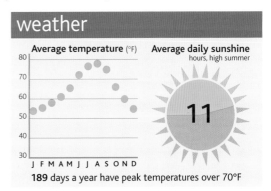

weather

Average temperature (°F)   Average daily sunshine
hours, high summer

11

J F M A M J J A S O N D
189 days a year have peak temperatures over 70°F

The town hall of Huelva fronts a delightful tree-lined square

Property

People living on the Spanish side of the border enjoy considerably lower prices, property included, than their neighbours in Portugal. It is quite usual to take advantage of the disparity by living in Spain and commuting daily to Portugal. However, property prices are rising. They took off at the start of the new millennium, rising on average by 10 per cent in 2001, 20 per cent in 2002 and another 20 per cent in 2003. That said, property prices in the 25 miles of true Spanish Algarve remain 30 per cent lower than Portugal to the west and the Costa del Sol much further east.

Types of property

Almost all properties are new builds. The boom in golf clubs and excellent sandy beaches along the Costa de la Luz are the driving forces behind many local property initiatives. However, the coastline has been spared mass development and remains much quieter than other costas. Local authorities keep tight control, imposing strict planning laws. For example, within this stretch of Spanish Algarve between Ayamonte and Huelva lies the picturesque town of El Portil. Five minutes away is Nuevo Portil, a beach/golf complex with two-bedroom apartments from £75,000 and three-bedroom linked townhouses, with gardens and communal pool, from £130,000. Villas with four or five bedrooms start at £250,000. There are neither shops nor bars. By contrast, the village of Villablanca, set amid orange groves ten minutes inland from Ayamonte, has new three-bedroom townhouses that blend in architecturally with local traditional whitewashed houses, close to shops and bars. They start at £75,000, with detached four-bedroom villas from £120,000. For those who enjoy town life, apartments in new three-storey blocks in Ayamonte begin at £72,000.

The biggest development along the coast is Isla Canela, a natural island four miles by two and a half. This fifteen-year building project has 3,500 properties planned for completion in 2010. At the moment, 60 per cent of owners are Spanish, the other 40 per cent mixed European, chiefly Portuguese – but increasingly British. Forty per cent of the island is protected wetland, and the rest is golf course, beaches, a marina and residential accommodation ranging from one-bedroom apartments to detached villas on golf course, beach or marina. All are sold off-plan to a waiting list of buyers.

interesting facts

❊ In 1492, Christopher Columbus set sail from Palos de la Frontera.

❊ The composer Manuel de Falla was born in Cádiz.

❊ The Lusitano horse of Andalucía originated over 25,000 years ago.

❊ The famous black fighting bulls of Spain are bred in the sierras around Cádiz.

❊ The imperial eagle and the lynx are two endangered species that survive in the Parque Nacional de Doñana.

What can you get for your money?

These price bands are a guide to the properties you might find.

Under £70,000	farmhouse needing renovation
£70–120,000	one- or two-bedroom beach/marina or golf apartment; or two-bedroom town apartment
£120–200,000	three- or four-bedroom detached villa, communal pool; or three-bedroom linked townhouse
£200,000+	luxury golf chalet with garden, own pool, etc.

Points to consider

So far, the trend among British buyers on the Spanish Algarve is towards second homes as an investment – used initially for a few weeks of the year for holidays and the rest of the year for rental income – with an eye to their owners retiring there full-time.

Ayamonte lies on the Guadiana river, the border between Spain and Portugal

The hinterland remains relatively unexplored by house-hunters, although this will change as the coast becomes increasingly popular. There is a slow trickle of foreigners into the villages, especially up the River Guadiana. But *fincas* rarely appear on the market, and when they do they usually need a lot doing to them.

You might buy an old three-bedroom farmhouse with a hectare of land for £80,000 and then spend another £40,000 to bring it up to scratch, including a new kitchen and bathroom. Always check on water and electricity supplies, and that there is a clear title to the land.

There is no coastal road direct from Huelva to Jerez and Cádiz. Instead you have to bypass the Doñana National Park by taking the motorway inland to Seville and then south to link up again with the Costa de la Luz. It all adds to the unique character of this corner of Spain.

budget flights & transport links

FLY TO FARO FROM:
East Midlands (Bmibaby)
London Stansted (easyJet)
Luton and Manchester
(Monarch)

FLY TO JEREZ DE LA FRONTERA FROM:
London Stansted (Ryanair)

A direct train runs from Madrid to Seville, then change for train to Huelva (the end of the line). Hire cars are available there.

The car ferry goes from Plymouth to Santander and Portsmouth to Bilbao (both on the north coast of Spain). From there, drive south through Spain, via Madrid and Seville and on to Huelva. Alternatively drive south through Portugal, via Lisbon motorways. Within the Spanish Algarve, there is limited public transport.

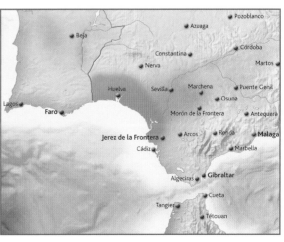

House-hunters

Bill and Linda Gilroy
Budget: £90,000

With their home in England already sold, London cabbie Bill Gilroy and his wife Linda, a secretary, were ready to move into their dream home abroad. Researching the property market in Spain on the Internet had persuaded Linda that the Spanish Algarve was the place for them: quiet, authentically Spanish and very good value for money. She had quite clear ideas what they were after. 'I'd like something "olde worlde," perhaps a *finca* with a tiny plot of land.' And Bill? 'If her indoors is happy, I'll be happy.'

Two-bedroom show flat in Isla Canela with two bathrooms, kitchen, open-plan living room. Sun terrace and access to two swimming pools and tennis courts. **£81,000**

Two-bedroom restored townhouse in Ayamonte with bathroom, kitchen, living room and artist's studio. Two patios and large roof terrace. **£92,000**

Property 1

The first property they saw was in Isla Canela. Bill and Linda visited a show flat on the Hoyo development, a series of complexes by the golf course. They immediately liked the way the exteriors of the buildings were painted in traditional earthy colours. Inside they found a light, well-proportioned flat with good-sized rooms. The terraces of the flats were all west-facing so they could be enjoyed in the evenings. On one side of the complex was a nature reserve and on the other the golf course, so all views would remain unobstructed. As well as the communal facilities of the urbanization, property owners could enjoy a 50 per cent reduction in the membership of the golf club. Family membership would amount to £3,800, considerably cheaper than the fees for clubs in neighbouring Portugal. The Gilroys liked it but felt that it was more of a holiday or weekend home.

Property 2

Further upriver, they saw a townhouse in the busy fishing port of Ayamonte. It had a large light living room with original fireplace, a second sitting area lit by a stained-glass skylight and complete with traditionally tiled water feature, and a small fitted kitchen. Upstairs there was a large mezzanine living area/study and a tiled roof terrace with views across the rooftops to the Guadiana river and Portugal. 'It's out of this world, unique, and with so much character.' The only potential problem was the damp in the upper floor. The water outlets on the flat roof were too small and partially blocked so the water had seeped into the floor below. Enlarging the outlets, a damp course and guttering would cost around £5,000 but the Gilroys could ask the owner to carry out the work as a condition of sale. However, they were not convinced that it was what they were looking for.

Property 3

They continued their search in the countryside outside Cádiz. Inside a traditional *finca*, the living area was open plan with three rooms arranged in a circle, linked by arches. The living room had traditional terracotta floor tiles and a working fireplace. A second reception room was being used as a study while the kitchen was big enough to include a dining area. Outside, the terraces had splendid views of the countryside while the 4,000 square metres of land included a grove of cork oaks and a typical Spanish barbecue. If Bill and Linda wanted a pool, it would cost about £10,000 but they would have to plan around the twelve protected oak trees. The other potential disadvantages were the lack of mains water (the house was supplied by its own well) and electricity, although a recent court case had overturned a local farmer's objections to pylons on his land. So electricity would be forthcoming – but when? That aside, the property was too remote for the Gilroys.

Three-bedroom finca near Cádiz with two reception rooms, bathroom, kitchen and dining area. Two terraces and 4,000 square metres of land. £64,000

Property 4

Two-bedroom modern villa outside Conil de la Frontera with bathroom, living room, dining room, kitchen and study. Two sun terraces, 1,350 square metre garden and separate guest apartment. £103,000

Finally they saw a modern villa outside the traditional town of Conil de la Frontera. It had been designed by the current owners to be light, roomy and simple. The original part of the property had been converted into a separate apartment, keeping the original wooden beams and fireplace. It could be used for rental income. Bill and Linda fell head over heels in love with it and determined to stretch their budget if they had to. They were warned that the property had been built without planning permission. The owners did however have land deeds that entitled them to whatever was on the land. All that was required was the services of a good solicitor to ensure that the property was registered with the land registry at a cost of £6,500. Despite advice to offer £96,000 because the villa had been on the market for three months, they went in at the asking price. Their offer was accepted and they were able to start their new life in the sun within a couple of short months.

Ex-pat experience

Peter and Cindy Van Hoof
Ayamonte, Spain

Their marriage, five years ago, meant a new start for Peter and Cindy Van Hoof. They uprooted from England and moved to the Costa del Sol where Cindy had previously lived and worked for four years. To begin with, they did little but joined the Salon Varieties, an amateur theatre group in Fuengirola. Then Cindy found a job with a company who ran lawn-green bowling holidays. It was on one of her forays for them that she discovered Ayamonte. 'I phoned Peter immediately and told him I'd found the place for us. It's twenty years behind the other *costas* with very little tourism, although that's changing now. The infrastructure is being developed with new roads and the building at the beach. Ayamonte's quiet marina is now stuffed with boats and they've built a new one at Punto Moral.'

> 'Always try to have at least a few basic words of Spanish. The rewards are numerous.'

It wasn't long before they found a run-down *finca* advertised in an insurance broker's window. Gradually they are doing it up and taming the 8,000 square metres of garden. Meanwhile Cindy became an estate agent. 'Eighteen months ago, I started helping an estate agent friend. Now there are eleven of us coping with more and more people coming over.' Peter eventually took over as manager of the bowling green at Isla Canela. From there he has moved to the Castro Marim Golf Club just over the border in Portugal. It is only a fifteen-minute drive to work but, because of the time difference between Spain and Portugal (an hour behind), if he leaves home at 8 a.m. he arrives at work at 7.15 a.m.! They have had no problems with the bureaucracy of living and working in Spain. 'Getting an NIE number can be a pain but our bank arranged for us to get one in Ayamonte so it was very straightforward. We haven't had any problems with the legal side of working here. The only oddity is that Peter pays Portuguese tax and I pay Spanish.'

> 'Integrate with the locals, the lifestyle, and sample food as much as possible.'

They have made a lot of Spanish friends, largely through Peter's love of bullfighting. He became a member of a bullfighting fraternity who support an up-and-coming local matador. One of Cindy's interests is music and she hopes to start a small theatrical group although, as yet, there are not enough ex-pats to join her. Apart from amateur dramatics, Peter has found time to indulge his enthusiasm for painting in watercolours and acrylics. Being close to Spanish people has been enough for them to get reasonably fluent in the language while enjoying the lifestyle. 'The diet here is far better with plenty of really fresh fruit and veg, and a great variety of fish. The cost of living must be one-third what it is in the UK. It's a much more relaxed way of life. You just drop down into first or second gear and stay there.' The only things they miss from the UK are their children and grandchildren.

Cindy outside her and Peter's home in Ayamonte

Hérault

Languedoc-Roussillon, France

Squeezed between Provence and the Pyrenees, Hérault provides the ideal alternative to some of the more traditional hot spots on the French Mediterranean coast. With the Pyrénées-Orientales, Aude, Gard and Lozère, it makes up the region of Languedoc-Roussillon. There are long stretches of beaches backed by large lagoons dotted with flamingos. It is a perfect environment for mastering watersports before venturing out into the Mediterranean.

Recent years have seen an increase in development, with resorts springing up around the small fishing villages – but without destroying their character. The Languedoc is the most prolific wine-producing region in France and inland, the coastal flats give way to a landscape of row upon row of vines. Further inland still, towards the mountain ranges of the Massif Central, rivers wind through a land of old villages and towns, with ancient remains and

The marina at Cap d'Agde provides some of the most desirable real estate on the coast

highlights

❈ Hiking in the Parc Naturel Régional du Haut Languedoc
❈ Drinking coffee in one of Montpellier's atmospheric squares
❈ Exploring Pézenas
❈ A leisurely boat trip down the Canal du Midi

websites

www.french-news.com
online edition of *The News*, France's English-language newspaper

www.cdt-herault.fr
official tourist board site

www.decouvertes-herault.fr information on Hérault and link to magazine

ruined castles, while the Canal du Midi is for those who like a leisurely chug in a narrowboat.

Once part of Occitania, a large region stretching from the Rhône to the Pyrenees whose people spoke the *langue d'Oc*, Languedoc-Roussillon has had a long history of different rulers, all of whom have left their legacies architecturally, agriculturally or culturally. Local cuisine is similar to that of neighbouring Provence, relying on olive oil, garlic, tomatoes and herbs. Naturally fish is a mainstay so the region is famed particularly for its *bouillabaisse du Languedoc* and *bourride de Sète* (fish stews), and its mussels and oysters from the Thau basin. Pézenas is renowned for its *petits pâtés* (lamb sweetmeats). Among the full-bodied wines of the region are Vin de Pays d'Oc, Corbières, Coteaux de Languedoc, Minervois and Faugères. The many colourful local festivals include the Bullfighting Festival (Bézier, August), the water jousting contests (Sète, August) and the Fishermen's Festival (Sète, July).

Where to go

The university town of **Montpellier** is the capital of Hérault, and indeed Languedoc. Its captivating historic centre has been pedestrianized, and seven-teenth- and eighteenth-century mansions restored. Every square has its share of cafes and bars, and the city has a vibrant, welcoming atmosphere and a thriving cultural life. **Béziers** is 50 miles away. A relaxed city known for its rugby matches and bullfights, it is dominated by the medieval Cathédrale St-Nazaire. **Pézenas** is another enchanting town with a rich architectural heritage so unspoilt it is frequently used for film sets (see Property 4, page 20). Several of Hérault's medieval villages are *'circulades'* (have a circular layout) and have become protected sites, among them **Alaigne**, **Alairac**, **Capendu**, **La Calmette**, **Fabrègues**, **Murviel-lès-Béziers** and **Puissalicon**. Further inland, the Parc Régional du Haut Languedoc offers an untamed mountainous region of river gorges, lakes, forests and wild rock formations. Isolated sheep farms, tiny hamlets and medieval villages can be found there as well as outstanding chances to walk, pothole and watch wildlife.

The coast was a wild stretch of lagoons and marshland until government investment brought about its transformation. The first of the new beach resorts was the futuristic and controversial **La Grande-Motte**, providing facilities for all watersports. The most important fishing and industrial port is **Sète**. Once an island, it is now joined to the mainland by a sandspit, separating the sea from the Bassin (lagoon) de Thau. The Grand Canal runs through the centre of the old town, flanked by beautiful Italianate houses, and meets the sea at the old port where there are plenty of restaurants serving up the day's catch. Eight beaches run in an almost unbroken chain to **Cap d'Agde**, the largest and busiest of the modern resorts, particularly known for its naturist colony. The development of the coastline has been environmentally considerate, so that Hérault is becoming more and more popular as people come in search of something less expensive but just as rewarding as its long-established neighbour.

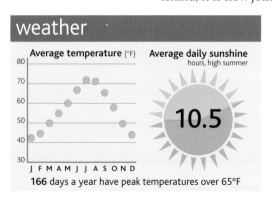

weather

Average temperature (°F)

Average daily sunshine
hours, high summer

10.5

J F M A M J J A S O N D

166 days a year have peak temperatures over 65°F

Property

Since the start of the millennium, house prices throughout Hérault have risen an average of 15–20 per cent annually, and considerably more in the most desirable areas. It is more affordable than Provence, but it is catching up fast. Agents currently depict it as a sellers' market that is pushing up prices. Not so long ago, British families with a typical budget of £100–200,000 could expect to buy an old and substantial character family house, with view, garden and room for a pool. No longer – £200–300,000 is closer to the mark.

A new-build house (perhaps a 'Spanish-style' villa), on a development on the edge of a town, will give you more for your money: £200,000 for a four-bedroom house with garden and pool, and quite often proximity to the beach. There is a regular supply of town and village houses on the market around that figure, but outside space, even small gardens and terraces, is a crucial factor in local pricing and stretches budgets accordingly. House-hunters often arrive with high hopes of land and views in the country, but end up settling for the charm of a village or small town.

The Canal du Midi flows through Sète to its fishing port where there is a rich mixture of quayside shops

Types of property

There is a wide variety of property on the coast and up through the plains and vineyards to the hills. Many require some work. It pays to be quick off the mark as the more attractive ones, in terms of character, location and price, tend to be snapped up very quickly. Characteristic features might include exposed stone, gently sloping terracotta roof and blue or green shutters.

A typical village house, such as those in the area particularly favoured by the British around Pézenas and Clermont-l'Hérault, is tall and narrow, with a garage at the lowest level, and living accommodation beginning on the first floor. There might be balconies with painted wrought-iron balustrades and, if you are very lucky, a roof terrace.

Points to consider

Location is of course an important consideration. There are small, modern, one-/two-bedroom apartments in Agde for about £30,000, but don't be surprised to pay double for their older equivalent in the more sought-after port of Sète further along the coast. You could buy a small village house for £60,000, but expect to pay 50 per cent more if it has a terrace or courtyard. They are hard to find, but if you come across a

interesting facts

❊ Béziers is the unofficial wine capital of France.

❊ The Languedoc region produces 40 per cent of France's wine.

❊ The playwright Molière and his actors performed for several seasons in Pézenas.

❊ The Canal du Midi, linking Sète with Toulouse, took 15,000 workers fourteen years to build.

❊ Hérault was named after the River Hérault that crosses the department from north to south.

complete wreck in a town or village for £50,000, you would need half as much again to make it habitable.

What can you get for your money?

These price bands are a guide to the properties you might find.

£30–50,000   one- or two-bedroom apartment in village, no terrace; or one- or two-bedroom apartment on coast with balcony; or three-bedroom village house needing major renovation

£50–80,000   five-bedroom old village house to renovate, no garden; or two-bedroom smart townhouse

£80–135,000   three-bedroom character house, terrace, but no pool or garden; or bigger character village/townhouse, courtyard or terrace; or five- or six-bedroom shell for complete restoration, land

£135–200,000   three-bedroom smart character house, small garden, pool space; or six-bedroom village/townhouse needing some work (possibly to divide into two), plus garden/terrace; or good location new villa, land, possibly pool

£200–350,000   large character house with land and pool; or four- or five-bedroom modern villa, plus pool/garden, near coast

£350,000+   smart five-bedroom village/townhouse, terrace or courtyard; or character house and buildings to restore, vineyard etc; or old large building complex needing work

One of the circular villages near Montpellier

budget flights & transport links

FLY TO MONTPELLIER, NIMES, CARCASSONE OR PERPIGNAN FROM:
London Stansted (Ryanair)

TGV train from Paris to Montpellier is three hours. Hérault is autoroute-friendly, especially from the north (e.g. Paris south to Clermont-Ferrand and then on the A75 autoroute south into Hérault and Montpellier). Another autoroute, the A9 running

east to west from Provence to Barcelona, is also easily approachable from two other autoroutes from the north. Inside Hérault, a car is essential, especially with air-conditioning in the summer months when roads get crowded along the coast.

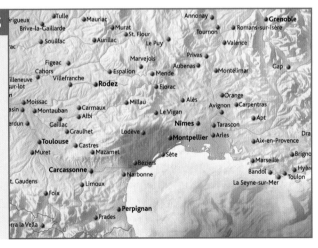

House-hunters

Keith and Elaine Short
Budget: £100,000

'The Côte d'Azur without attitude' is what Keith and Elaine Short were hoping to find when they visited the South of France. They were looking for a holiday home that would eventually become their bolthole for six months of the year when they got a little older. Although Keith had been a builder, he had no intention of buying somewhere to renovate. They had dreams of somewhere big enough for their family to be able to visit them, without a garden but with a patio or terrace where they could enjoy the sun and eat outside. If they found the right property, they were prepared to push up their budget.

Property 1

They first visited the busy marina of Cap d'Agde, where largely modern property blocks are built up round eight marinas. Small flats were available for £50,000 but demand was outstripping supply, so the Shorts would have to act quickly if they saw something they liked. The town benefits

from an aquatic leisure park, sandy beaches and plenty of cafés and shops. The apartment they saw was very small but painted in subtle pastel shades making the most of the space. The kitchen was compact, the living room was small with a marble floor that led into a loggia overlooking the marina. The downstairs bedroom was again on the small side but did have lots of storage room. Upstairs the master bedroom was fresh and airy with its own tiny secluded terrace. The size of the apartment was more than compensated for by its location. In the high season, they could rent it for £500 a week (less 15 per cent to a rental agency who would deal with all the details). However, Keith and Elaine did not want to rent and the apartment was far too small for their family to visit comfortably.

Two-bedroom apartment overlooking the marina in Cap d'Agde, with open-plan kitchen/living room, bathroom. Two terraces, car parking space. **£92,000**

Two-bedroom house near the beach with open-plan living/dining room, kitchen, two bathrooms. Front and back gardens and patio. **£92,000**

Property 2

Further down the coast they saw a house set back from the street with its own front and back gardens. It was a peaceful location and a pleasant house with a south-facing living/dining room that caught the sun all day. Its tiled floor made it cool in summer but there was a wood-burning stove for chilly winter nights. The kitchen was fully fitted with cabinets made from local oak. The large master bedroom had a modern ensuite bathroom and both bedrooms were well supplied with fitted cupboards. Outside there were various fruit trees giving shade to the garden. The Shorts liked it. 'It's been very well maintained, though if the kitchen and living room were knocked through it would seem

Three-bedroom vineyard retreat with open-plan living room, kitchen, office. Terrace and pool. £112,000

bigger. We'd probably cut down a few of the fruit trees at the back and extend the patio.' Keith and Elaine were not worried that the house was in a designated flood area. The last flood had been in 1993 and had only reached the end of the street. Although it was advertised as a 'beach house', it was twenty miles inland – too far from the beach for their grandchildren.

Property 3

They continued their search inland among the vineyards. A fifteen-year old house built in traditional style complete with tiled roof and blue shutters offered a good-sized living room with a cool tiled floor. The modern kitchen was brand new and even boasted an indoor barbecue. Outside the plunge pool glimmered in the sun next to a shower and bar. 'This is the exact layout we're looking for. We love the tiles and the space. The three bedrooms give us plenty of space for visiting family too. It's a marvellous house for entertaining.' Despite liking the property a great deal, however, they felt that it was in the wrong location for them – again, too far inland.

Property 4

Finally they travelled to Pézenas, once the administrative centre of the region – which means that it has an extraordinary collection of mansions built between the fourteenth and eighteenth centuries. Seventy of them are listed and many retain their distinctive features of arcaded courtyards and external staircases. This architecture has spilled into the hamlets and villages in the surrounding countryside. It was in one of these miniature versions of Pézenas that they saw the next property. An old corner house had been completely renovated to provide a comfortable family home. The big open kitchen had tremendous French charm, combining traditional detail with the convenience of modern fittings. The living

Renovated four-bedroom house near Pézenas with two bathrooms, kitchen, living room. Two balconies and garage.

£70,000

room was large and light with added character from a wood-burning stove. The master bedroom was another good-sized room with fireplace and view of the town square. The attic room would make an ideal nursery for Keith and Elaine's two grandchildren. The barn was used as a garage that had room for two or three cars, while on the floor above was a massive unused room. Both the Shorts could see the potential and the price meant that they would have capital left over to carry out the work, but it was a much larger project than they were prepared to undertake in retirement from the building trade.

They agreed that the area was perfect for them but they had just seen the wrong properties. They wanted somewhere close enough to the beach for the grandchildren, without a car journey to get there. Their search was not over but their enthusiasm was undiminished.

Ex-pat experience

Tony and Carol Tidswell
Nizas, Hérault

All the Tidswells – from left to right, Carole, Tony, Alexandra, Jack and Miranda

It was the British education system that drove Tony and Carol Tidswell and their two young children to France. 'Children can start school when they are two here, so by the time compulsory education begins at six, the early schooling gives them a huge advantage especially when it comes to reading and writing. Education is exceptionally good until after the baccalauréat, although universities here are no worse than in the rest of the world.'

What began as a short-term experiment outside Lyon turned into a permanent arrangement when, after four years, they decided to move south to buy a house and a dog. They fell in love with a derelict property that was largely built in the eighteenth century but included a chunk of tenth-century fortress and village wall, and a section from the fourteenth century. It had thirty-six rooms ripe for renovation that had not been touched since 1926, and had no electricity or plumbing. They bought it for 'next to nothing' and over the next five years, Tony and Carol lived off their capital while they did it up virtually by themselves. 'We thought we'd have a B&B but three days was enough. Anyone retiring here to do that must be mad. It's extremely hard work.' Instead Tony turned to his computer and now manages an online rental company (www.rentalsfrance.com) of over 1,000 French holiday properties and runs a newsletter at the associated www.francevoila.com that advises on everything to do with living in France. 'We had to make a living because in France you do pay more taxes, but the benefits you get are much better than those in England.'

'Always ask a French professional how things should be done.'

'Do not deal with unregistered property agents. You could end up losing your house or, at worst, in jail.'

The Tidswells were made welcome by the local community who would come to watch and help work on the house. It is also an extremely safe environment. 'American friends were initially horrified when we let our three-year-old out of sight. There's a joke that this is the only country in the world where muggers say please and thank you! The people are even nicer than we imagined.'

They have everything they need in their village of 500 people. Recently a new supermarket joined the library, school and café-bar. Otherwise there are regular visits from the travelling barber and butcher, and vans selling fish and horse-meat. The worst thing Tony has experienced is the amount of bureaucracy. 'It can get on top of you but everything is done to a pattern and there is usually a way round it if, rather than stubbornly trying to do it your way, you ask advice from the relevant person.' That aside, they came with expectations of a better quality of life and better education for their children and that is exactly what they have got.

The Campo de Gibraltar

Andalucía, Spain

The great rock of Gibraltar overshadows the town's marina

Only nine miles from Africa, the Campo de Gibraltar is the part of Spain that borders Britain's famed landmark, the rock of Gibraltar. It enjoys both Atlantic and Mediterranean coastlines: one more rugged and windy, the other a calmer sunbather's haven. Inland, there are dramatic mountain ranges, dense woodland and picturesque hill-top villages. The Parque Natural de los Alcornocales provides opportunities for all sorts of outdoor activities, including walking, biking, caving, climbing and horseriding, and watersports on the reservoirs. The coast is a paradise for windsurfers, while whale- and dolphin-watching trips run from Tarifa and Gibraltar. Back from the coast, there are manicured international golf courses at Sotogrande and San Roque.

In the south of Cádiz province, this area is as rich in history as the rest of Andalucía. The Bronze Age tombs dug into the rock face at Algeciras, the prehistoric cave paintings near Jimena de la Frontera, the ruined Roman town of Baelo Claudio at the coastal resort of Bolonia, the ruined forts and the white Moorish villages – all are legacies of the civilizations that by being here kept a toehold in Europe.

The local cuisine is heavy on fish and shellfish – from cuttlefish, squid and sardines to tuna, swordfish and fried cod. Game is popular inland and unusually there is an edible thistle, *la tagarnina*, used in stews. A different spin is given to some dishes using Moroccan influences. Numerous festivals take place throughout the year, including the Fiesta de la Tagarnina (Los Barrios, February), the Féria Real, celebrations and bullfighting (Algeciras, June), and Velada y Fiestas de 'La Salvaora' (La Línea, July).

Where to go

The wealthy resort of **Sotogrande** is known for its expensive property, glamorous marina lined with fish restaurants, and its top-class golf courses, polo fields and tennis courts. Moving towards Gibraltar, the coastline is wilder and less developed. The old town of **San Roque**, founded by Gibraltarians fleeing the British in 1704, is typically Andalucían, with steep narrow streets and Moorish-style houses climbing up to the Mirador that commands a view to the Rock. **La Línea** is right on the Spanish–British border. A modern town has sprung up around the original fishing village, so at its heart is the area round the harbour and church where many of the original buildings are preserved. Thought to be one of the sunniest towns in Spain, it has developed as a tourist resort over recent years.

The Rock of Gibraltar divides the town's two sandy beaches. On the other side of the bay from Gibraltar lies **Algeciras**, originally named Al-Yacirat-Aljadra or 'green island' by the Moors. Green it is not. Now predominantly a port and industrial town, there is little to keep the visitor. **Tarifa** is the first town of note on the Atlantic coast. Its white-sanded beaches and windy shoreline have made it a magnet for the world's windsurfers, so prices are high. The charming walled old town, entered through the Puerta de Jerez, retains its Moorish air with twisting streets, whitewashed houses and ancient Castillo de Guzmán.

Perhaps the greatest attractions of the region lie inland, in the Parque Natural de los Alcornocales. Named after the cork oaks that flourish there, there are many narrow river valleys giving rise to lush vegetation. At its south-western tip is the atmospheric market town of **Los Barrios**, ideally situated between the attractions of inland and the coast. Further inland are the Moorish frontier towns of **Castellar de la Frontera** and **Jimena de la Frontera**. In 1971, the population of the former was moved to a new town near Almoraima. Some moved back but many homes were taken over by German and Dutch hippies. Jimena de la Frontera is also a pretty white town with a large defensive castle, but it is particularly well sited.

highlights

❊ The Parque Natural de los Alcornocales

❊ Sporting facilities at Sotogrande

❊ Whale and dolphin watching

❊ Windsurfing on the Atlantic coast

websites

www.straitsnews.com news and information service in English for the Campo de Gibraltar region

www.nabss.org British schools in Spain, including Sotogrande

www.123propertynews.com online magazine with property and related issues in southern Spain

www.tuspain.com useful online guide to buying property and living in Spain

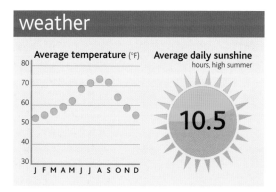

weather

Average temperature (°F)

Average daily sunshine — hours, high summer

10.5

Property

Some of the jewels of the Campo de Gibraltar, such as the 5,000-acre Sotogrande resort with its Valderrama championship course and a 600-pupil international school, come with price tags to match – a million pounds for a marina townhouse, riverside apartment or golf fairway villa is not unheard of. The house-hunters arriving with an £80,000 budget, expecting to find a detached three-bedroom villa on the coast, face disappointment. It might have been a reasonable sum a couple of years ago, but not today. Some properties close to beaches near Tarifa, for example, have doubled in price in four years, and £100,000 is considered a minimum entry-level budget for a decent family seaside home.

With coastal prices spiralling, mid-range house-hunters today increasingly focus on inland properties – whether in the countryside or in towns and villages – where they can buy double the amount of bricks, mortar and land than they can on the coast. Many settle in one of the southern Moorish-style white villages and towns that perch on rugged hillsides throughout the region.

Types of property

In a typical white village or town, the dazzling terraced houses – two, three or four storeys high, thick-walled and often whitewashed annually – line narrow, twisting and cobbled streets brightly spotted with pots of geraniums. Exterior stone steps may lead up to sun terraces or a flat roof which can be used for either sun-bathing or drying washing. Inside, bedrooms often lead from one into another. Overlooking the street there are usually small balconies, with wrought-iron balustrades. In taller buildings, the ground floor may contain a garage. A common feature is a communal patio, shared with adjoining houses, with an orange or lemon tree for shade.

There is a still a wide range of other properties, with prices to match, through-out the seven municipalities of Campo de Gibraltar. Some properties are ready to move into. Some need a lick of paint and improvements to bathroom and kitchen. For those who enjoy a challenge, there are old abandoned ruins, in both village and country, requiring a complete rebuild. Such properties might cost £40,000 to purchase and the same again at least to do up from scratch, but you could end up with a magnificent three- or four-bedroom house in a superb and spacious setting.

The southernmost town of Tarifa was first established in the tenth century and has 24 miles of fine sandy beaches within easy reach

What can you get for your money?

These price bands show the properties you might find.

Under £50,000	three-bedroom townhouse needing renovation; or ruin needing total rebuild
£50–90,000	three-bedroom farmhouse; or three-bedroom terraced townhouse; or large ruin, with land to build separate property
£90–150,000	four-bedroom detached country house with pool and garden; or smart four-bedroom townhouse with patio/terrace
£150–250,000	four-bedroom villa near beach, garden, parking, pool; or large country farmhouse with outbuildings, several hectares
£250,000+	luxury resort villa, own pool, all mod cons; or luxury resort/marina penthouse

Points to consider

As with so much of Andalucía, there was a rural exodus towards life in the towns. Now new life is being breathed into the white villages again with foreign buyers keen to live there – the phrase 'the new Tuscany' has even been bandied about.

Jimena de la Frontera is much favoured by the British and Irish. At the turn of the new century, it was reckoned that 400 foreign families lived in the area. This figure has now doubled – and so have prices, although they are still cheaper than back home in the UK.

Small towns, perched above steep river gorges, overlook miles of vegetable gardens, olive groves, cork forests, vineyards and horse and bull ranches. The better houses here are much sought after, with cheaper prices falling slightly to the west towards Cádiz. Some are holiday homes, and others are permanent residences for ex-pats working in the area, especially with Gibraltar a short drive away.

The property that house-hunters Adrian and Patricia chose – a two-bedroom apartment overlooking a golf course (see page 27)

budget flights & transport links

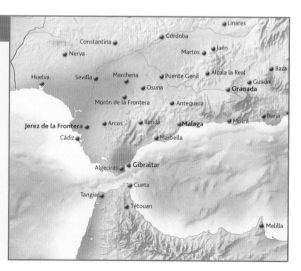

FLY TO MALAGA FROM:
Bristol, Liverpool, London Luton, London Stansted (easyJet)
London Gatwick (easyJet, Monarch)
East Midlands (easyJet, Bmibaby)
Southampton (Flybe)
Manchester, Cardiff (Bmibaby)
Dublin (Ryanair)

FLY TO JEREZ FROM:
London Stansted (Ryanair)

FLY TO GIBRALTAR FROM:
London Luton (Monarch)

Trains run direct from Madrid to Algeciras. Within the area, there are local trains (e.g. Algeciras to Ronda), often stopping at stations some distance from villages. Buses tend to be school and once-a-day transport. A car is almost essential for country living, although motorways are being improved and lengthened all the time. There are now new motorways almost all the way from Málaga to Algeciras and also from Jerez to Algeciras.

House-hunters

Adrian and Patricia Taylor
Budget: £100,000

Patricia had been planning to retire to Spain but, when she met Adrian, a builder, her plans were put on hold. After ten years together, they finally decided to find a place in southern Spain where they could lead a less stressful life and spend more time together. With friends in nearby Estepona who knew people in the building trade, Adrian had a good chance of finding work quickly.

Property 1

The first place they visited was the resort of Sabinillas. Just outside town was a fourth-floor seaside apartment in a cosmopolitan urbanization. Morning sun lit the dining area in the light and simply decorated spacious living room. A narrow sun terrace would be ideal for morning coffee or evening drinks. Adrian lit up at the sight of a second bedroom used as a study, but Patricia reminded him they would need it to accommodate the many relatives and friends who were already queuing up to stay. They loved the location, the superb communal pool and the surrounding landscaped gardens, and were surprised to hear the community charge was as low as £45 a month (10 per cent less if paid in annual instalments). The urbanization was composed of a mixed community of British, Spanish and Scandinavians who held regular management meetings and social get-togethers. The only downside was the lack of parking facilities, although the Taylors could rent a nearby garage for £40 a month. However, after living in a house for so long, they decided that being surrounded above and below by other people was not ideal.

Three-bedroom seaside apartment with living room, bathroom and modern kitchen. Sun terrace and communal pool. **£75,000**

Three-bedroom finca *in the Parque Natural de los Alcornocales with living room, kitchen and bathroom. Sun terrace, outbuilding, pool and one hectare of land.* **£92,000**

Property 2

They continued their search in the Parque Natural de los Alcornocales, where they looked at an eight-year-old *finca*. The open-plan living room and kitchen needed some updating. The kitchen had an open wood-burning fireplace, and all three bedrooms had great views across the countryside. Outside there was a spacious sun terrace finished with terracotta tiles, and a pool filled with natural spring water used to irrigate the land that came with the property. The land was very fertile, with various fruit trees and vines, and also included a chicken coop. The verdict: 'We could live the good life here and you could walk and walk for miles. We loved it.'

Adrian and Patricia were amused to know they could earn £750 a year from the crop of a ton and a half of chestnuts. The property had a well in addition to the source of spring water. To use the pool for swimming, they would need a pump and filter system that would cost around £2,000.

Although they loved the property, ultimately they felt it would be too remote for them as a permanent home.

Property 3

Next was a townhouse in the centre of the small town of San Roque. Built in 1816, its modest traditional façade was deceptive – inside were as many as fifteen rooms. The house had been owned by several generations of the same family, who had most recently divided it into three apartments. It had the potential for redivision to give one self-contained apartment that would earn a rental income of £350 a month. There was a slight camber to the floors but nothing to worry about. The building was struc-

turally sound – just its age made it a bit crooked. Although the property had masses of potential, Adrian and Patricia were not convinced it was for them. 'Neither of us had seen anything like it but it didn't have the outside space we wanted.'

Three-bedroom townhouse in San Roque with two living rooms, three kitchens, dining area and study. Courtyard and sun terrace. £68,000

Property 4

Lastly they saw a modern architect-designed villa close to the beach in Bahía de Casares. The south-facing living room had a large open fire and a good view through French windows to the garden. The master bedroom, with ensuite bathroom, led on to a sun terrace with views across to the sea. The mature garden had been well cared for, although Adrian proposed planting flowers for colour among the shrubs. As far as Patricia was concerned, the pool was the icing on the cake. 'This was all we asked for and more.' The community included various Scandinavian, British, German, Spanish and Gibraltarian home-owners,

Two-bedroom modern villa in Bahía de Casares with open-plan living area, kitchen and bathroom. Private garden, communal garden and pool. **£115,000**

many of them permanent residents, who organized various social gatherings and management meetings, so there would be plenty of opportunity to meet the neighbours. Adrian and Patricia stretched their budget to offer £105,000 but they were refused.

Determined to find a new home, they continued their search and found a two-bedroom apartment overlooking a nearby golf course (see page 25). They have since moved to Spain and are settling into their new life abroad.

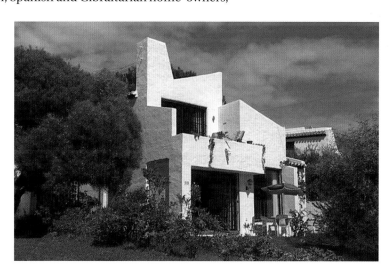

Ex-pat experience

Lynne and Neville Stock
Estepona, Spain

A two-hour each way commute between Surrey and London took its toll on Lynne and Neville Stock. Eventually they decided to sell up and to move to Spain. 'Maybe we were naive but we thought if we didn't do it then, we'd never do it.' By that stage, their son was working but Anna, their twenty-one-year-old daughter, decided to come too.

The previous year they had spent New Year in Marbella and decided that while they did not want to be part of a huge ex-pat community, neither did they want to go to the mountains where they felt they would cope less well. Estepona offered them exactly the right combination: up-and-coming but with a population at least 80 per cent Spanish. It meant they had to take language lessons immediately: 'We still struggle but can just about get by at a basic level.'

> 'Be prepared to kiss away two or three hours just waiting in the bank for a statement.'

The next problem was how to earn a living. Lynne had been a nurse back home but, without the language, she could not continue in her profession, so they decided to buy a large house to convert into holiday apartments or four or five individual apartments. 'We bought an apartment overlooking the marina to let while we rented a three-bedroom house to live in. Then we found a large villa that had been neglected for the past fifteen years. We had heard horror stories about Spanish builders but had to bite the bullet and hired some recommended to us. They have been superb.' The house has been converted into four luxury apartments for rent, with one other for themselves so clients will receive five-star treatment (www.theextramileholidays.com). Meanwhile Anna works as a nanny for visiting families, although will eventually help in the family business.

After just two years, the Stocks have already seen changes. 'There had only been one two-star hotel in Estepona. Now they're building two five-star ones with another close by. The amount of apartment building is phenomenal and the increase in traffic has led to a new underground car park now.' The bureaucracy has been time-consuming to deal with but they are anxious that their business should be completely above board. 'We'll certainly be paying tax. We don't believe in using the facilities of a country and not contributing towards them.'

> 'You must have an NIE number [Spanish National Insurance] to buy property.'

Their lives have changed hugely since leaving British shores. 'We hardly watch TV. We eat later like the Spaniards. Although we're not sporty, we live a much more outdoor life without lying on the beach. We've got used to the attitude of *mañana* and go with the flow. Although we miss theatres, Málaga is only an hour away with all sorts of cultural things going on.' Lynne says she misses family, friends and Boots the Chemist but, 'Do we regret moving? Not one bit.'

Campania

Western Italy

ampania marks the start of the Italian Mezzogiorno: the land of the midday sun. Located on the west coast, directly south of Lazio, Campania offers a Mediterranean climate and a dramatic coastline, particularly from the Amalfi seaboard southwards, while the islands of Ischia, Capri and Procida are stunning alternatives. Inland there are well-cultivated plains in the north, but farming land to the south is interrupted by imposing mountain ranges with the volcano Vesuvius just south of Naples.

The ancient Romans first saw the area's potential as a holiday resort. They dubbed it *campania felix* or 'pleasant country', and built seaside villas and estates there. There are a number of ancient sites to be explored, the most famous being Pompei, Herculaneum and Paestum. Classical myths live on – the Lago Averno was believed to be the entrance to Hades, and it was on these shores that Ulysses ordered his crew to tie him to the mast of his ship so he could hear the sirens' song without succumbing to their temptation.

The vertiginous Campania coastline is renowned for its spectacularly sited towns and villages

highlights

❋ The petrified ruins of Pompeii
❋ Greek temples at the ancient city of Paestum
❋ The Blue Grotto of Capri
❋ The Bourbon Palace at Caserta
❋ The view of the Amalfi coast from hill-top Ravello

websites

www.deliciousitaly.com has links to local tourist offices in Campania and to information on the region

www.englishyellowpages. it is a guide to English-speaking professional organizations and businesses in Italy, region-by-region

Over the centuries, Campania fell under different rulers from the Normans to the Spanish and French until Garibaldi defeated the Bourbons in 1860 for the kingdom of Italy.

Campania is famous for its cuisine, particularly for its reputation for having invented the pizza. Naturally, pasta dishes are always high on the menu too and can be washed down with one of the local wines such as Lacrima Cristi, Fiano di Avellino, Gragnano or Taurasi. Around Paestum, farming land is used for grazing herds of Indian water buffaloes brought to Campania in the sixteenth century and kept for their milk – an essential ingredient of the famous buffalo mozzarella. There are plenty of festivals celebrated in the region, among them the Festivals of San Gennaro (May/September/December), Madonna del Carmine (July), Madonna di Piedigrotti (December) in Naples and of course the Sorrento film festival (November).

Where to go

Naples is the hectic capital city of the region, superbly positioned on the Bay of Naples. The German playwright Goethe is reputed to have said 'See Naples and die' – a reference to its beauty, not to the legendary death-defying behind-the-wheel tactics of Italian drivers. It is a large, sprawling city with a lively historical centre; a wealth of churches, a medieval university, palaces and monasteries stand beside busy street markets, cafes and restaurants.

Further south are the wealthy resorts of **Sorrento**, **Amalfi** and **Positano**, linked by the winding corniche that provides an exhilarating drive with truly spectacular views. Sorrento is the last town of note in the Bay of Naples and has attracted foreign visitors, including Ibsen, Wagner and Maxim Gorky, for hundreds of years. Round the peninsula, steep cliffs plunge into the sea, but perched above them are some of the most desirable and expensive pieces of real estate to be found in Italy. Thanks to their vertiginous locations, the towns' potential for modern expansion is severely limited. Amalfi, with its tenth-century Duomo, has been popular with the British since Edwardian times when wealthier members of society wintered there. Positano is arguably the most beautiful, with its steep streets, colourful houses and chic shops. A little inland is **Ravello**, the hillside village crowning one of the coastal mountains with a superb view out to sea.

Further south still, near the vibrant port of **Salerno**, lies the Parco Nazionale del Cilento e Vallo di Diano, the second-largest park in Italy, occupying 450,000 acres of land and 60 miles of coastline. For hundreds of years the Cilento coast was raided by pirates, so every mile the locals built a fortress – many of which survive today. Inside the park are a series of rocky cliffs and hill-top villages, where traditional ways of life remain untouched by the demands of the twenty-first century. On the coast, life is quieter, with smaller resorts, fishing villages and white sandy beaches.

weather

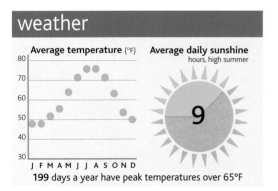

Average temperature (°F)

Average daily sunshine
hours, high summer

9

199 days a year have peak temperatures over 65°F

Property

Some of the most expensive properties are to be found along the Amalfi coast where the pastel-hued and white-washed houses are often made of stone hewn from the cliffs to which they cling so precipitously. From above, they form a mosaic of different shades of terracotta-tiled roofs, and pots of flowers and tubs of lemon trees crowding the balconies. *Vietri*, the local brightly coloured tiles used on every possible surface, are everywhere. More affordable are the coastal villages and towns further south, such as Agropoli where an apartment with two main rooms, in a three-story character building in the old town, can cost as little as £15–20,000 and require not much more than modernisation and a lick of paint.

Inland is a landscape of limestone rocks dotted with patches of fertile soil which becomes increasingly barren the higher you go. Here a *rudere*, a small tumbledown peasant cottage built of *pietra viva* (local stone) falls within the same price range but will need total renovation to provide two bedrooms, living room, kitchen and bathroom. It is usually more practical to renovate, which is encouraged, rather than wait for planning permission to knock down and build again. With local agriculture in decline, surrounding land with olive and lemon trees and vines, is reasonably cheap. A growing trend is *agriturismo* where larger farmhouses are turned into accomodation and restaurants, with local produce on the menu.

With Capri only three miles away, the Massa Lubrense has nearly twenty miles of coastline in the middle of the protected marine area of Punta Campanella

Types of property

On the coast, think expensive (very). Property in the more desirable parts of Naples can cost as much if not more than Rome while prices along the coast erupt volcanically as wealthy Neapolitans snap up second homes. Inland, behind the coastal strip, think bargain prices, especially in more arid mountainous areas. Always make sure there is a reserve water tank.

Allow £350–500 per square metre for any restoration by local builders, including work on walls, floors and roofs. Comparable country properties cost about 40 per cent more in Umbria and considerably more in Tuscany. Prices have risen 10–15 per cent over two years, increasing substantially towards the coast. A two-bedroom apartment with balcony in Naples or Salerno can cost £200,000, plus another £35,000 for a prime sea view.

interesting facts

* Toto, the late, great screen comic and star of 100 movies, was a native of Naples.

* Greta Garbo and Jackie Kennedy holidayed on the Amalfi coast.

* American wit and writer Gore Vidal called his house in Ravello 'the best place to observe the end of the world'.

* Pompei and Paestum are Italy's two most visited archaeological sites.

What can you get for your money?

These price bands sgow the sort of property you might find in a rural area.

£15–20,000	small two- or three-roomed farmhouse in need of complete renovation
£20–25,000	bigger farmhouse, major work needed
£25–30,000	medium farmhouse, ready for occupation
£35–55,000	detached restored house or farm, one hectare of land
£55–70,000	modern villa, one hectare of land
£70–80,000	large modern house with four or five rooms on each floor
£85–135,000	top-of-the-range villa, two storeys, plus attic and basement, good location, two hectares of land

Points to consider

The old fishing village of Positano has been transformed into one of the Amalfi coast's most popular resorts

It is hard to find local property advertisements aimed at north Europeans, or local property websites with an English translation. Indeed, most estate agents here have only a smattering of English, if any. Always proceed with caution. Make sure everything is legal, then check again. Avoid common pitfalls by checking the vendor is the legal owner and that a house, extension or pool has had planning permission (penalties include at best a fine, at worst demolition). A *rudere* can only be legally rebuilt on its footprint, despite any owner's claim to the contrary. Planning permission on building land can take forever to come through despite indications otherwise. Always check service charges and shared costs for apartment block flats, which may be brushed aside during purchase. The golden rule throughout the whole region is to ask questions, check documents at the town hall, make sure all legalities are watertight, and ask again.

However, despite the caveats, there is a warm welcome for those who successfully negotiate the local property maze. And despite warnings of corruption, the streets are much safer than in Britain.

budget flights & transport links

FLY TO NAPLES FROM:
London Stansted (easyJet)

Naples is the hub for all major air, road and rail links into Campania. Main railway lines run north to Rome, east to Bari and south to Reggio Calabria. The main A1 motorway runs from Rome south to Naples, with the A3 running from Naples to Salerno and into the Cilento, and the N18 branching off it to run down the coast.

Internally, district railway lines connect with even the smallest towns throughout the province. Buses are good but a car is essential in the country. Local roads are bad, especially at night.

House-hunters

Mark and Ali Lodge
Budget: £150,000

Running a pub is a demanding life, so Mark and Ali Lodge were bent on finding somewhere they could relax, that would be big enough for entertaining friends and perhaps with a pool. They had chosen to look in Campania because they thought it would be warm in January and February when their business is quiet and they can more easily get away.

Property 1

The first house they saw was just outside Positano. Spread over two storeys, it had a large open living room with a bar, a huge table, fireplace and plenty of space. The wooden fitted kitchen had space for a small breakfast table and even had a built-in radio. The master bedroom was idiosyncratically decorated with hand-carved painted furniture and an elaborate mosquito net over the bed. The house had become too big for the elderly owner, who wanted to move quickly but without dropping the price. Not having enough room for all her furniture in her new place, she was prepared to sell some of it with the house. Bearing in mind its high sentimental value and the fact that much of it was hand-carved, she was asking £10,000 for the furniture.

Two-bedroom sea-view retreat outside Positano with two bathrooms and three reception rooms. Two balconies, a sun terrace and garage. £146,000

The verdict? 'The whole house is great for a party and has lots of character. We like some of the furniture but perhaps we could negotiate over which pieces to buy. We could move in tomorrow if it weren't for the decorating eccentricities.'

Property 2

Three-bedroom hillside house near Paestum with three bathrooms, living room and dining room. Large roof-top terrace with valley views and pool. £116,000

Next, they travelled inland to see a hillside house close to Paestum. Recently renovated, it had a new tiled floor in the light and airy dining room and a similarly light living room complete with fireplace, built-in cupboards and a fridge – handy for a beer. The kitchen was small but compact and led out on to the patio. Upstairs the master bedroom had superb views through the French windows across the countryside. The pool was big enough for swimming rather than just a quick plunge. This property had the outside space that Mark and Ali wanted without being at all overlooked. The snag lay with the pool, in that the previous owner had not applied for planning permission – a typical omission in this part of the world. Either Mark and Ali could take the risk of it not being found out or they could pay a fine of between £500 and £1,500 to legalize matters.

Property 3

They moved on to the Cilento National Park where the deserted tenth-century village of San Severino offered one house that had been restored. Behind its ivy-covered medieval exterior, the property was in good condition. The modern kitchen with fitted wooden cabinets and new appliances led into an open-plan living/dining room with a brick fireplace. Outside there was a terrace with great views of the ancient viaduct in the valley below. Upstairs the bedrooms were good sizes and there was a basic shower room. A huge roof terrace ran the length of the house and caught the sun all day long. The house was simply decorated and in a unique position, but Mark and Ali felt it was a bit too remote and could imagine the villagers below looking up to see what 'the lunatics on the hill' were up to.

Two-bedroom house in San Severino with living room, dining room, kitchen and shower room. Two terraces. £126,000

Property 4

Lastly they visited a luxury modern villa close to the picturesque fishing village of Santa Maria di Castellabate. Property is expensive here and does not stay on the market long but, only a short drive inland, money does go further. The large white-painted living room had stripped floors, and plenty of room for the existing furniture and more. The big picture windows were a great asset. The fully fitted kitchen was attractively untraditional, the master bedroom had a vast picture window to show off the sensational view and a perfect ensuite bathroom with a big whirlpool bath. A huge terrace led off a round bedroom in the tower and, by the garden, a long veranda made an ideal place for eating and entertaining all summer long. The outside of the house had been left unpainted simply because the owners had been unable to agree on a colour for the last ten years. As far as Mark and Ali were concerned, 'This place oozes quality. It's to die for.' They could see themselves living there but the house was beyond their budget. A possible solution would be to get it to pay for itself by renting it out in the summer. It should fetch £550 per week unless they added a pool, in which case it could command as much as £800.

Luxury five-bedroom villa outside Santa Maria di Castellabate with seven bathrooms, living room, dining room, office and garage. Two balconies, terrace and 4,000 square metres of land.
£195,000

Mark and Ali went home to look at their finances but, as they reviewed things, they realized that the weather during the winter months when they were going to be able to visit most was not going to be warm enough for them. Reluctantly giving up their opportunity for this house, they instead fulfilled a life-long love affair with India and bought a house in Goa.

Ex-pat experience

Angus Kirk
Agropoli, Campania

Angus Kirk with his sons, David and Michael

After completing a degree and working in a building society for a year, Angus Kirk decided to teach English as a foreign language, not too far from home – 'I thought of it as a one-year thing before I got a real job.' Twelve years later he is still there, running his own English school, married to his Italian wife, Antonella; they have two sons, David, four and Michael, one. 'I first lived in Salerno, which is about the size of Coventry with plenty to do,' says Angus. 'I met lots of nice people and decided to stay another year.' He moved to Agropoli, a small seaside town, where he has been ever since. 'The weather is exceptional here, and it's very quiet – our first cinema has just opened. Most things revolve round Salerno, forty-five minutes away, where there are nightclubs, a multi-screen cinema, restaurants, pubs and so on.'

Evenings are centred on the *passeggiata*, when everyone takes to the streets for a walk before supper, and the bars. 'But not in the sense of drink as much as possible. I've never seen anyone drunk here except myself! I quickly realized that I couldn't do that any more because people look at you after two pints.' Another big thing is *agriturismo* (farmhouse cooking with good fresh ingredients) and of course there's the beach. 'You could spend every day there from May till October.'

When Angus arrived in Italy he could speak three words, *pizza, pasta* and *ciao*. However, he found that the language was quite easy to pick up, especially from watching television. Now his children are brought up speaking Italian and attending the local schools. 'Kindergarten is fantastic. Elementary school is good but after that middle school is a bit of a black hole, partly because of the age, partly because of overcrowding and partly because the teaching could be better.'

> 'Check the paperwork ten times with ten different people.'

He found buying their house a minefield. 'Agents' fees are high at 3 per cent to buy and 3 per cent to sell. You must check how your house is described on the deeds. If previous owners extended or changed the use without permission you may find yourself with a property liable for demolition or having to pay the *condono* (a fee to the government) to cover it.' He found it impossible to get hold of a property that was 100 per cent legal. When buying, tax is paid on the declared value of the house, not the purchase price. At the notary's, he found himself paying two cheques – one for the declared value and one for the balance of the asking price, paid when the notary's back was deliberately turned.

Little has changed since he moved there. The town is 'continually changing its mayor' and corruption at a national level is almost a way of life. However, the pluses to life in Italy are many. 'The importance of the family; the weather does make a difference; the food is excellent; people are really friendly; we're by the sea; I enjoy the local festivals which are a good way of exploring the villages; there's no violence.'

> 'It's better to buy an already renovated property than have to tussle with builders.'

Although Angus and his family enjoy visiting the UK, there is no question that Italy is now his home and that will not change.

How to buy a property in Italy
A general guide

Italian law does go a long way to protecting foreign property buyers but, as with every country, it is advisable to seek your own independent legal advice before you sign anything or transfer money.

The role of a *geometra*
Having found the property but before signing the preliminary contract (*compromesso*), you will need to conduct a survey and local searches, and check that the property conforms with local planning and building regulations. Properties in Italy are not automatically surveyed before a purchase. However, for your own peace of mind, it is wise to appoint an architect/surveyor (*geometra*) who will not only be able to survey the property and provide you with a written report, but can also plan any alterations with you, submitting them for approval and overseeing the work.

Exchanging contracts
The preliminary contract can be drawn up by the vendor, the estate agent, a notary or a lawyer. This document should include the terms of the sale: details of the property, the seller and buyer, the price, how the purchase will be financed, completion date and details of any other conditions (such as the buyer being able to obtain a mortgage or planning permission, or the discovery of local plans to build something that will affect the property) that have to be completed before the sale. At this stage a deposit (*caparra* or *deposito*) of anything between 10 and 30 per cent is payable to the seller. Make sure you are absolutely clear about the terms of the deposit and whether and under what circumstances it might be returned.

It is possible to register the *compromesso* with the local registration tax office. This has the advantage of preventing another prospective buyer getting involved because he will be informed of the existence of your *compromesso* when they conduct local searches. You will need to make sure that the property is in the condition you saw it when you made your original offer and includes everything you agreed to buy. Make a visit with your lawyer to check. Consult your lawyer and/or estate agent about the declaration of value that is normally less than the purchase price and is set by the local registry and *commune*.

Completing contracts
By the time you are ready to complete, you must have fulfilled all the conditions in the contract and obtained an Italian Tax Code Number (*codice fiscale*). Completion must take place in front of a notary (*notaio*) appointed and paid for by the buyer. A notary is an independent representative of the government who has the authority to transfer legal title to properties. If the buyer is not fluent in Italian, then an officially accredited interpreter must be present or, alternatively, the buyer must give power of attorney to his lawyer or estate agent. Before signing, the balance of the money payable by the buyer (including the notary's fee and any relevant taxes) must be presented, preferably in the form of a banker's draft. After signing, the property is yours.

Registration
All that remains is for the notary to register the change of ownership at the land registry. The buyer should collect a copy of the purchase deed from the notary's office a couple of weeks later. The notary will provide the buyer with a form with which to notify the local police of the purchase. After this, you should contact the mains suppliers, notifying them of the change in the property's ownership – and then you can sit back and enjoy it.

Murcia

South-east Spain

Murcia has one of the least visited stretches of Spanish coastline. Known as the *Costa Cálida*, 'the warm coast', it has 155 miles of beaches stretching between its boundaries with Almería and Alicante. Local authorities have resisted the demands of mass tourism to ensure their seafronts remain unspoilt. Another bonus is the northern Mar Menor, a vast natural lagoon where the water is slightly warmer than the Mediterranean and has therapeutic properties. It is an ideal spot for swimming and other watersports. Here the strip of land known as La Manga divides the lagoon from the Mediterranean. Popular with tourists, there are high-rise hotels, golf courses, a casino and an extensive marina, along with the lively nightlife. Two regional parks worth noting are the Parque Regional de Salinas de San Pedro, known for

The coastline near the resort of Aguilas remains remarkably unspoilt and boasts some good dive sites

its salt pans and the flocks of migrating flamingos, and the Parque Regional de Calblanque where the natural beauty of the coastline south of La Manga is preserved intact. Here the coastline becomes more rugged, featuring dramatic cliffs and rocky coves, some of them accessible only by boat. The name Murcia comes from the Latin word for mulberry, the staple diet of silk worms. The region was known for its silk production from Roman times until the mid-twentieth century.

Cuisine focuses on the local vegetable produce and fish from the coast. Specialities include *caldero* (soupy rice with peppers and fish), *paella hurtana* (a rice dish using various vegetables) and plenty of grilled and salt-baked fish. Local handicrafts include ceramics from Totana, glassware, basketware and rush matting and textiles. The fiesta of the Moors and Christians is celebrated throughout the region, along with other celebrations such as the Spring Festival and spectacular Holy Week parades.

Where to go

The principal coastal town is **Cartagena**, a strategic port for Carthaginians and Romans onwards. Ancient remains are dotted around town, including its ruined castle. South of **Puerto de Mazarrón**, a resort favoured by many Spaniards for their holiday homes, the coast becomes wilder until reaching the last resort of **Aguilas**. Once a Roman fishing port, the town with its fifteenth-century castle provides a gateway to various pleasant beaches.

The capital of the region, **Murcia**, was founded by the Moors who irrigated the surrounding land, creating the *huerta*, otherwise known as 'the garden of Spain' where all kinds of vegetables are grown. A university town, its centre is the eighteenth-century square, La Glorieta. Murcia also boasts a particularly fine cathedral and various museums.

Small farming villages are scattered throughout the region, most of them of Moorish origin. **Lorca** is one of the prettiest and played a frontier role in the Moorish–Christian battles. Its ruined fortress remains but the centre of town is the Plaza España, bordered by elegant stone buildings including the Colegiata de San Patricio (Church of St Patrick). Further north, **Caravaca de la Cruz** is particularly known for its castle housing the Santuario de la Vera Cruz. Cehegín, another attractive town, spans the length of a street running between two cathedrals. The town has a number of beautiful seventeenth-century mansions dating back to when it was dominated by wine merchants. The well-preserved town of **Moratalla**, with its confusion of steep streets and brightly painted houses, is set high on a plateau surrounded by fertile land. **Totana** is a farming town whose narrow streets come alive every Wednesday, market day. **Alhama de Murcia** hunkers down on the fringes of the Sierra Espuña, one of Murcia's beauty spots. The scenery here is breathtaking, with rocky ridges crowned by ancient hill-top towns and villages, many of which survive through rural tourism. Keen to encourage this, the Spanish Tourist Board will authorize grants to restore old buildings for holidaymakers.

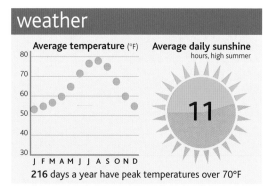

weather

Average temperature (°F)   **Average daily sunshine**
                                     hours, high summer

11

J F M A M J J A S O N D
216 days a year have peak temperatures over 70°F

Property

Until recently, Murcia was a little-known region for British house-hunters. However, times are changing. There are newly built motorways and marinas, golf courses and housing developments, with more at the planning stage. Throughout the region, property prices have doubled on average. But despite this hive of activity, and the concomitant hike in property prices, Murcia and its *Costa Cálida* remains relatively cheap compared to neighbouring regions and relatively unspoilt.

Property-wise and topographically, the *Costa Cálida* is divided by Cartagena, the region's second city. To the north, the coast is considerably more developed, particularly round the Mar Menor. Other developments are mushrooming in this touristy area: more high-rise blocks, villa estates and golf courses. A typical price here is about £45,000 for a one-bedroom apartment (and £10,000 for each extra bedroom) for those buying sun, sea and sports rather than the real Spain.

To the south of Cartagena, there is a scarcity of property for sale or land to build on between the resorts of Mazarrón and Aguilas. In general, prices for properties on the coast have risen 25 per cent in two years, and there have been tales of a 400 per cent rise in the cost of prime building land near the sea in one year.

Types of property

A typical traditional country dwelling, in need of some minor work, is often a one-storey house, with thick whitewashed walls, a red/orange or mottled yellow tiled roof, and pale terracotta floor tiles. There might be a bread oven outside and a large fireplace in the living room where the cooking was done. Installing a new bathroom and kitchen is usually the first priority for new owners, and perhaps rearranging rooms so that the second and third bedrooms are not reached through the first.

There are village and townhouses, some of which appear quite small and in need of a lick of paint on the outside, but smart and spacious inside with lots of rooms leading off the main living room. Large seventeenth- to nineteenth-century town mansion houses, or *casas senoriales*, with wrought-iron balconies and family coats of arms, are also found. Some are enormous, with over 25 rooms, and are major renovation projects, perhaps for someone with a business in mind. Good-sized *cortijos* with vineyards attached to them can also be tracked down.

Inland, there are plenty of undisturbed historic villages, such as Herbeset

Sunset over the Mar Menor

What can you get for your money?

These price bands are a guide to the properties you might find.

£35–45,000	5,000 square metres building land (allow £400 per square metre building costs)
£35–55,000	medium-sized country ruin in need of complete renovation
£40–65,000	two-bedroom apartment in coastal complex
£55–100,000	two- or three-bedroom country/village house needing minor work
£90–165,000	new/nearly new house on outskirts of town
£100–150,000	two- or three-bedroom country/village house, renovated; or three-bedroom villa with pool in cheaper area
£120–165,000	new three-bedroom villa, garden, terrace, carport, near Mar Menor
£200–400,000	big mansion townhouse, often in need of renovation; or luxury three-bedroom villa and pool at La Manga resort

Points to consider

A number of British home-owners in coastal resorts have upped sticks after as little as two years and moved to inland Murcia, attracted both by cheaper prices and a quieter, more Spanish lifestyle. Inland, there are ruins and semi-ruins, often with considerable amounts of land, from £40,000. A complete rebuild could double the price, and you might need to bring in water and electricity. As a rule of thumb, the further you go inland, the greater the bargains to be found – and authentic Spain, rather than tourist villages.

budget flights & transport links

FLY TO MURCIA FROM:
Southampton (Flybe)
East Midlands, Manchester (Bmibaby)
London Stansted (Ryanair)

FLY TO ALICANTE FROM:
London Gatwick, London Luton (easyJet, Monarch)
Bristol, Liverpool, London Stansted, Newcastle (easyJet)
East Midlands (easyJet, Bmibaby)
Manchester (Monarch, Bmibaby)
Cardiff (Bmibaby)

A new airport is planned near Murcia city, which is also the hub for fast rail transport into the region. The N330/A7 motorway runs from the south connecting Murcia with Alicante and towns further north, as well as with Madrid. The N332 runs along the coast with the N301 motorway linking the Mar Menor to Murcia City. Other main roads are being improved all the time, and public transport within the region is cheap and good, although a car is essential in the country.

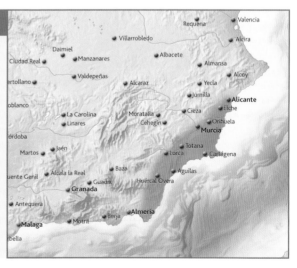

House-hunters

Eamon and Claire Belton
Budget: £140,000

The Beltons are an extended family of ten who enjoy holidaying together. With this in mind, Eamon and his daughter Claire had decided to look for a holiday home that would have something to offer all of them. Spain had been a popular holiday destination for the family and they thought that they would get better value for money if they went to Murcia. 'We'd like to find somewhere big enough for the family, preferably an older property with a bit of character and outside space, ideally with a pool.'

Property 1

They began their search in the Campo Cartegena, where citrus groves and olive trees stretch to the horizon. Within the enticingly named Sun Valley there was a new development where they looked round one of the properties that had already been sold to see if they wanted to have an identical one built. The rooms were good sizes with air-conditioning and ceiling fans. The kitchen had plenty of work surfaces and storage space with a separate utility room doubling as a wine store. All the bedrooms had ensuite bathrooms. Most impressive of all was the enormous sun terrace with its beautiful pool. The Beltons were impressed. 'The rooms were all big and bright. There won't be any fighting over who sleeps where.' As they would be buying off-plan they could redesign the house to include another bedroom provided the property remained on the planned footprint. To have the garden professionally landscaped would cost £6,000 unless Eamon's father-in-law did the work. It might be as long as another fifteen years before the development was completed and at least a couple before the services were completed.

Three-bedroom modern villa with three bathrooms, open-plan living/dining room and kitchen. Private swimming pool, roof terrace, patio and garden.
£129,000

Two-bedroom historic townhouse in Cehegín with two reception rooms, kitchen/dining room, bathroom, attic for renovation and top storey annexe. Covered roof terrace and patio. **£59,000**

Property 2

The next property was a seventeenth-century town-house in Cehegín that had been renovated a year earlier. Many original features had been retained, including the wine cellars and wine press, original beams and arched ceilings. Although the exterior looked narrow, the interior opened up into a spacious living area with an enormous kitchen, once part of the cellar system. With only two bedrooms, there was the possibility to convert the attic into two more, plus a bathroom and glazing in the open

Three-bedroom cottage in Gebas, Sierra Espuña, with two bathrooms, living/dining room, kitchen. Patio, mature garden and two-room chalet. **£89,000**

terrace room to make a fifth, at a cost of between £8,000 and £10,000. The other snag was that water had leaked through the roof into the timbers and walls below. Either they could replace the tiles and waterproof the roof every four to five years (£2,500) or they could replace the timber with concrete beams and retile completely for a permanent solution (£8,000). Eamon thought it better to sacrifice the beams than the rest of the house beneath.

Property 3

Next they visited the Sierra Espuña where a restored village house in Gebas offered a large living room with exposed stone walls and original beams and fireplace. The flagstone floor led into a fully fitted modern kitchen and a large double bedroom and ensuite bathroom. Upstairs there were two more bedrooms with exposed beams and wonderful views. The guest chalet was currently used as a laundry and storeroom but could be adapted into guest accommodation for about £6,000. Outside, the patio and landscaped garden even had a bread oven, and there was another patch of land over the road. This was the rural look that Eamon had hoped for. 'It's tastefully restored with plenty of space and a lovely outside area for a barbecue.' To site a pool over the road would cost about £9,500. Although the village did feel cut off, the baker calls daily, there is a summer restaurant and a supermarket a couple of miles away. In the summer, the rental potential was good – £130 a weekend and £350 a week.

Property 4

Four-bedroom villa in Los Alcázares with living room, dining room, kitchen, two bathrooms (including jacuzzi). Guest studio room with shower. Summer house with open-plan living/kitchen/bedroom and bathroom. Pool, garage, garden, terrace. **£168,000**

Los Alcázares on the Mar Menor was once frequented by the Moors. It has retained its charms as a fishing village since the major developments have been kept to La Manga. The property came with three living spaces: the villa, the top floor studio and the summer house, all of it extremely spacious and light. The Beltons loved it. 'It's a stunning house, perfect for us. So much attention has been paid to the detail.' Although it was over their budget, they could rent rooms for an income of £5,000 over the summer. The furniture was included in the price but could be sold for around £11,000. Planning permission had been granted for another golf club in the area so the unsightly neighbouring land would be landscaped as the approach to the club.

Eamon decided that he would try to persuade his father-in-law to share the cost of the villa. His arm-twisting was unsuccessful but instead he made an offer on the townhouse in Cehegín. However, when he took his wife Denise to see it, she was not impressed. In the end, they decided to withdraw the offer and continue their search until they found something that they both liked equally.

Ex-pat experience

Peter and Jacqui Wright
Cehegín, Murcia

Accountant Peter Wright and his wife, Jacqui, were already disillusioned with living in Britain when, five and half years ago, he was offered a retirement package that was too good to refuse. 'At that time we had no particular love for Spain, having only seen the tourist developments on the coast. On the other hand, it was only a two-hour flight, so our four children would easily be able to visit.' They decided to take a couple of inspection trips. The second was to the *Costa Cálida*. 'Most people seem to want a piece of England in the sun but we were determined to find a detached country farmhouse away from the urbanizations on the coast.'

First, they renovated a farmhouse near Torre Pacheco, sold it, and moved to Fuente Alamo near Mazarrón to do it again. 'It was very good for me because I learnt to do it better the second time round. Eventually we sold that too because of the influx of British and the consequent development that came with them, and we moved inland to Cehegín.'

When the Wrights arrived, they took Spanish lessons for a year. 'It gave us a good basis, but the best learning curve was having to use it in the bars and shops and with our neighbours.' Then Peter took a job labouring on various sites to understand the different methods used. 'I've found that British people, because they cannot speak Spanish, prefer to employ other British when they are renovating property and as a result can pay at least three times the going rate. If you don't speak Spanish or keep in with the community, it's easy not to realize what you should be paying.' Now he and his wife have set up a business helping people who have recently moved to the area. 'The people who tend to live in this part love it for its beauty, its community, and its way of life, be it fiesta or siesta. I help by putting them in touch with Spanish builders. Then I monitor their project, as well as assisting with fitted kitchen purchases, furniture and so on. We aim to help people integrate into Spanish society.'

'Never trust anyone just because they are English. Be wary. We found a terrific agent here in Cehegín, who assisted us greatly in our move to the area. But not all are what they seem.'

'Make sure you are not under-financed. Many people leave after a couple of years, discovering things aren't always as cheap as they'd expected.'

The Wrights themselves settled swiftly into their new life. 'The Spanish are a very vibrant people with a great outlook on life. The three most important things to them are the health service, the education system and their quality of life. They work hard but not for work's sake. Their play is more important. We have loved every moment here and intend to stay for the rest of our lives.' Both Peter and Jacqui have experienced the health service first hand and were impressed with its speed and efficiency. Another bonus is the low crime rate. They have integrated so thoroughly that the only things they miss from England are their children and grandchildren.

Asturias

Northern Spain

The town beach of Ribadesella, Playa de Santa Marina has a stunning mountain backdrop. The old town and fishing harbour are on the other side of the estuary

Asturias has a lush, green, magnificent landscape with some 200 miles of untouched coastline known as the *Costa Verde*. Its other principal attraction is the Picos de Europa, the jagged mountain peaks thought to be so called because they were the first sign of European land seen by sailors travelling back from the New World. The vast Parque Nacional de los Picos de Europa offers outstanding opportunities for all sorts of outdoor activities, from hiking, biking and riding to climbing, skiing and watching birds and animals. In August, Arriondas is the starting point for the international canoeing races of the River Sella to Ribatedella. The surrounding rugged landscape, from snow-capped peaks to tiny villages huddled in lush verdant valleys, is hard to beat.

Being isolated by mountain ranges, Asturias has a unique history. In 718 the Visigoths defeated the Moors at the Battle of Covadonga and so established the first Christian kingdom in Muslim Spain. The legacy is seen in the many pre-Romanesque buildings and their language, Bable, which can still be heard in remote mountain districts.

Traditional festivities are held throughout the year. *Romerías* (pilgrimages) and *espichas* (cider celebrations) fill the summer months, while among the best-known annual fiestas are the Fiesta del Pastor (Cangas de Onís, July), Nuestra Señora de Covadonga (September), La Descarga (Cangas del Narcea, July), Fiesta de los Huevos Pintos (Pola de Siero, Easter) and Gijón's Cider Festival (August). Local cuisine is simple country fare, including such dishes as *fabada* (stew of beans, sausage and pork), *pote asturiano* (rich meat and vegetable soup), *caldereta* (fish stew), and a wide variety of fish, local cheeses and pastries. The most popular drink of the region is cider, with some wine produced in the west.

highlights

❋ Exploring the Picos de Europa
❋ Asturian pre-Romanesque churches
❋ Cave paintings at Tito Bustillo near Ribadesella
❋ Covadonga lakes (beware summer traffic)
❋ Drinking cider in one of the many *sidrerías*

Where to go

The principal cities of the region are **Oviedo** and **Gijón**. Oviedo is a university town situated on a plain where a number of well-to-do towns interrupt the surrounding apple orchards and meadows. The medieval part of the city contains its gothic cathedral and a number of pre-Romanesque buildings, and its main breathing space is the central Parque de San Francisco. The city has been the region's economic centre ever since the coal-mining days of the nineteenth century. Outside are the two churches of Santa María de Naranco and San Miguel de Lillo, both UNESCO World Heritage sites. The industrial port of Gijón is a vibrant modern city, with an old town that has been pedestrianized.

websites

www.asturiaspicosdeeuropa.com
general tourist guide to the region

www.asturcon.net
includes a comprehensive listing of 295 estate agencies and links to their websites

www.infoasturias.com
thorough journey through the region with detailed information

Along the coast are plenty of fishing villages that have retained their historic charm. The rocky shoreline is cut by narrow estuaries (*rías*), often with coves and fishing villages tucked into the inlets. **Llanes** is the largest resort east of Gijón. An attractive fishing village, it is the focus for many excellent beaches and is a short drive from the Picos de Europa. **Ribadesella** straddles the Sella estuary, and still boasts a number of elegant houses built at the turn of the century when the town was particularly popular. It is flanked by a number of little beaches. **Lastres** is another seaside village with staggered houses built into the steep hill, overlooking Colunga beach. **Villaviciosa** is a more prosperous town at the centre of the cider industry and is close to two beaches at Rodiles and Tazones. West of Gijón, the coast is less crowded. Among many other unspoilt fishing villages, **Cudillero** is the most delightful. The painted houses tumble higgledy-piggledy down to the harbour with plenty of narrow streets and stairways in which a visitor can get lost.

Apart from the Picos de Europa, inland Asturias has another nature reserve, the Parque Natural de Somiedo, where brown bears and wolves roam free. The countryside is stunning though fairly inaccessible without a car. Green valleys, wooded hills, lush meadows and craggy cliffs hide remote hamlets and peaceful villages.

weather

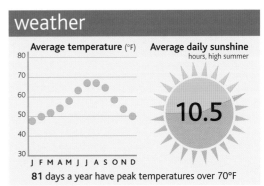

Average temperature (°F)

Average daily sunshine
hours, high summer

10.5

J F M A M J J A S O N D
81 days a year have peak temperatures over 70°F

The coast near Gijón, a lively modern city and the largest in the region

Property

The Germans and the British are leading the northern Europeans' discovery of the property market in Asturias. As elsewhere in Spain, property prices shot up just before the euro came in. Depending on the area, agents report rises of anything between 30 and 75 per cent over the past three years, although prices are stabilizing now. The majority of holiday homes are by the sea, the most popular strip being in the eastern half of the region between Llanes and Villaviciosa. Its advantages are its proximity to the airport and ferry port at Bilbao, and its easy accessibility to the Parque Nacional de Picos de Europa. Most home-buyers prefer to seek out traditional properties, but these can be relatively expensive. This has led to the spread of new builds in the traditional style.

Types of property

A typical Asturian house is built in stone, often left exposed but sometimes rendered with a strip at ground level painted a contrasting colour. It may have wrought-iron grilles over the windows, or shutters. One distinguishing feature is a projecting first-floor wooden balcony or corridor that may extend across a central section or the whole of the front of the house. Sometimes it is large enough to need the support of stone columns, so creating a shelter beneath it. Above, the typically gable or pyramidal slate or tiled roof has wide eaves that extend over the balcony, protecting it from the elements. On some of the grander homes nearer the coast, the balconies can be glassed in to extend an upstairs room as well as letting in plenty of light. Other notable properties are the *palacios indianos*, grand houses built by Asturian adventurers returning home, often with tell-tale palm trees in the garden.

Another feature frequently found in this region is the *horreo*, a wood and stone granary on stilts built separately from the house. Farmhouses may be joined to outbuildings such as a cow shed or barn. Inside there are frequently wooden floors, exposed ceiling beams and original fireplaces.

What can you get for your money?

These price bands are a guide to the properties you might find.

£25–40,000	country house needing renovation; or two-bedroom traditional village house in good condition; or 1,250-square-metre building plot in mountains
£40–£60,000	two-bedroom apartment in Gijón; or 1,250-square-metre building plot with sea views
£60–80,000	typical two-bedroom Asturian mountain house; or large *finca* for restoration with land
£80–100,000	old stone farmhouse with two bedrooms; or townhouse with small garden
£100–150,000	two-bedroom house with sea views; or better quality stone farmhouse
£200,000+	three- to four-bedroom house with sea views; or *palacio indiano* for restoration

The Picos de Europa mountain range is a big draw for outdoor lovers in Asturias

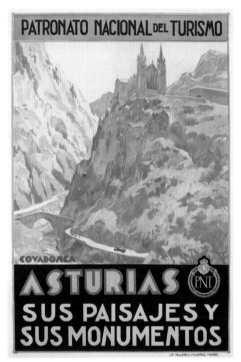

Points to consider

Bear in mind that prices for properties on the coast are virtually double those of equivalent-sized properties in the mountains. On the coast, you can expect to find all mod cons. If you buy further inland, most old houses do have services – if not, it should not be difficult to get the municipality to install them. The fee will naturally depend on the location of the house and how far it is from the nearest mains services. Most villages have a bar that also sells essential supplies, but there are vans that travel from village to village selling all sorts of goods – bread, meat, fish and so on. If you are anxious about entrusting your child to the local school, the English School of Asturias between Oviedo and Gijón offers a bilingual education in Spanish and English covering GCSE and A level syllabuses, and has bus routes to the main towns.

budget flights & transport links

FLY TO BILBAO FROM:
London Stansted (easyJet)

Brittany Ferries sail twice weekly from Plymouth to Santander. The ALSA bus service runs between Gijón west to Navia with further services inland to Villayón three times a week. The FEVE train service runs from Bilbao to Ferrol (Galicia) via Gijón. The principal road through the region is the N634, which runs along the coast from A Coruña towards Santander, diverting inland to Oviedo. The A66 motorway from León links Oviedo with Gijón and Avilés. Otherwise, inland roads tend to run parallel with the valleys south to north. A car is essential for travelling inland.

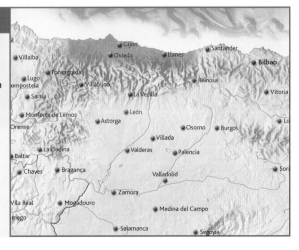

House-hunters

Pauline Andrew and Joe McKenna

Budget: £90,000

A love of the great outdoors took Pauline Andrew and Joe McKenna in search of a holiday home off the beaten track. They were game for finding something to renovate, since they both love doing up houses. As an ex-builder, Joe is good at renovating while Pauline's skill lies in being able to see if there is potential for a palace in a pile of rubble.

Four-bedroom hillside villa in the Picos de Europa with kitchen, living room, scullery and lounge. Three cellars, stable and 2,000 square metres of land. **£52,000**

Property 1

Their search began in the Picos de Europa where, in the tiny mountain village of Bodez, there was a hillside villa in need of renovation. A stable door opened into a large light hall. The living room had attractive wooden floors and ceiling, while the big old kitchen needed completely refitting. Upstairs there was a typical Asturian corridor, or glassed-in balcony, complete with bluebirds' nest for good luck. Downstairs was a large cellar once used for animals so the heat of their bodies would rise to warm the floor above. Pauline and Jo thought the place was 'breathtaking'. The original panelling and shutters were a bonus. A local builder quoted a price of £60,000 to renovate the whole place but, if Joe did some of the work himself, the price would naturally be reduced. He was encouraged to hear there was an excellent local timber merchant and that a nearby house, smaller but similar, had recently been renovated and sold for £245,000.

Property 2

Next they travelled to the fishing village of Cudillero, once known as the 'village of health' thanks to its production of medicinal fish oils. Today over half the town's population still makes a living from the sea. Just outside the village was a traditional fisherman's cottage in a hamlet. The house had been in the same family for over 200 years but had been recently renovated. The front door led into the new fitted kitchen and on to the dining room. It had all been decorated in neutral shades that made the most of the space and light. The basement had been turned into a large and comfortable

Renovated three-bedroom fisherman's cottage near Cudillero with bathroom, kitchen/diner and large basement. 2,000 square metres of land, with horreo. **£90,000**

living area, while outside the wooden *horreo* had potential as a summerhouse. Pauline and Joe were knocked out by the magnificent views and thought the basement might even be converted into a self-contained flatlet for visitors. However, on reflection, they felt that the internal layout did not work for them as a whole.

Property 3

They continued their search on the coast by the unspoilt Colunga beach. Overlooking it is the cliff-top town of Lastres, where they saw a stone townhouse. It had been lovingly restored over the last three years, using traditional Spanish building materials. The large living room had exposed stone walls and tiled floors. The kitchen was modern and fully equipped, with views across to Lastres port. Next door was a small tiled bathroom. The master bedroom also had exposed stone walls, while the attic space had been converted into an open-plan bedroom with sitting area and ensuite bathroom. Skylights ensured the room was bright and welcoming. The walled garden had been well cared for and even included a garden shed. This time Pauline and Jo were 'overwhelmed'. 'You could just put your clothes in the wardrobe and you've got a life immediately.'

Renovated three-bedroom townhouse in Lastres with two bathrooms, kitchen, living room with balcony, and open-plan attic. Walled garden. **£127,000**

Property 4

Their final port of call was the abandoned village of Priedamo in the Picos de Europa. This was a real find. The first house they looked in had a living room full of trophies attesting to the cheese-making prowess of the farmers. The kitchen had a tiled floor and a traditional farmhouse cooker, but otherwise needed completely refitting. The bath was outside. The second house, like the first, had electricity but also needed complete renovation. What appealed to both Joe and Pauline was the beauty of the location and the peace and quiet. However, it was a massive project to take on and they felt it was far more than they wanted.

A village in the Picos de Europa consisting of three three-bedroom cottages, six barns, two horreos, *several stone animal shelters and 12 hectares of land.* **£128,000**

Their deliberations led them to making an offer of £30,000 for the hillside villa in Bodez that they felt just had the edge over the others. Unfortunately the property had been inherited by a brother and sister, only one of whom really wanted to sell. Not wanting to wait until the situation was resolved, Joe and Pauline decided to pull out and look for something less fraught with complications.

Costa del Azahar

Community of Valencia, south-east Spain

The coastline of the Costa del Azahar offers plenty of fine sandy beaches

The Costa del Azahar is named after the orange blossom that flowers twice a year – its ninety miles of unspoilt coastline is the biggest orange-producing area in Europe. It lies just north of the Costa Blanca and has some of the cleanest beaches in the Mediterranean. It stretches the length of the province of Castellón in the Community of Valencia, from Vinarós in the north to Almera in the south, and some consider it extends further south to include Valencia town and beyond. This is where the Spaniards holiday. It is much more traditional, less crowded and considerably cheaper than neighbouring Costa Blanca.

Along the coast there are busy resorts and fishing villages, modern developments and ancient towns, while offshore lies the archipelago of the Columbrets that has recently been designated a protected Natural Park. Inland, the landscape is dry and mountainous, characterized by the terraces left by the Moors.

The area is particularly known for its production of ceramics and textiles, with wood-carving, basketware and rush matting, wrought-iron and leatherware coming close behind. Provincial cuisine depends on fish, shellfish and vegetables from the coast, with richer dishes of lamb, pork and game from further inland. One of the most typical dishes is *arroz a banda*, a combination of rice, fish, potatoes and garlic, while a speciality of the region is the truffles from Morella. Throughout the year there are plenty of traditional festivals, among them La Tomatina (Buñol, August), a giant tomato fight, and Las Fallas (Valencia, March), a riot of bonfires and fireworks.

highlights

❋ Fortified town of Morella
❋ El Maestrazgo – landscape and villages
❋ The old town of Peñíscola
❋ Caves at Vall d'Uixo
❋ Magnificent unspoilt beaches and clean seas

Where to go

Valencia is the third-largest city in Spain, with a vibrancy and warmth of its own. A strategic port founded by the Romans and much fought over by the Moors, it was finally absorbed into the kingdom of Aragón in the thirteenth century. It boasts a number of splendid historic buildings, including its cathedral, the Torres de Serranos, a triumphal arch built in the old city walls, and La Lonja, now a UNESCO World Heritage site. These are more than matched by the modern Ciutat de los Artes i de la Ciencia, some of whose buildings are still under construction. Since 1982, when it became the capital of the region, the city has been improved immeasurably.

Further north the coastal towns of historical note are **Sagunt**, **Castelló de la Plana** and **Peñíscola**, but the coastline is better known these days for its popular resorts such as **Vinarós**, **Benicarló**, **Orpesa**, **Benicàssim** and **Borriana**. The beaches offer long uninterrupted stretches of golden sand and clear aquamarine waters. Although Peñíscola is surrounded by a sprawl of modern development, the historic town has been preserved within its walls complete with cobbled streets, whitewashed houses and castle. All these are backed by the *huerta*, a fertile plain that is one of Europe's most developed agricultural regions supplying citrus fruits, vegetables, rice, corn, apricots, olives, almonds and much more.

El Maestrat is the rugged area inland from Peñíscola, with plenty of medieval villages. The most spectacularly preserved is the walled town of **Morella**, which rises to the castle on the rock above. Other noteworthy towns are **Forcall**, **Todolella**, **Castellfort**, **Albocásser** and **Ares del Maestre**. There are a number of attractive small towns further south that particularly draw summer holiday-makers in search of the slightly cooler climate, spa waters and plenty of outdoor activities. Popular towns are **Altura**, **Jérica**, **Viver Lucena del Cid** and **Montanejos**.

websites

www.valencialife.net
online English-language daily newspaper, *Valencia Life*

www.whichspain.com
useful info and how-to, including property matters

www.tourspain.es official site of the Spanish tourist board

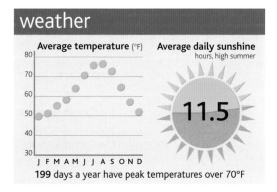

weather

Average temperature (°F)

Average daily sunshine
hours, high summer

11.5

J F M A M J J A S O N D
199 days a year have peak temperatures over 70°F

Property

Living in the inland village of San Juan would give a taste of authentic rural Spain

The coast immediately north of Valencia is dominated almost entirely by the Spanish, many of whom commute to the city for work. So far, it has not proved popular among expatriate homeowners. But beyond the city of Castelló lies a stretch of coastline that is a conservation area. Here, in and around the towns of Alcossebre and Las Fuentes – which enjoy a healthy climate, sandy beaches, a new marina and championship golf courses – an enlightened local planning authority legislates against building above three storeys. It releases pockets of building land only every few years, but such is the demand that people are willing to buy property off-plan and wait until it becomes available. They may pay 10–15 per cent more than equivalent property on the Costa Blanca further south, but overall prices are in keeping with the more sought-after parts of Spain. This is the up-and-coming area in the Costa del Azahar. Prices have risen about 20 per cent annually over the past few years, again on a par with much of Spain. If you want to move here, be prepared to pay £50–65,000 for a one-bedroom, off-plan apartment, to £90,000 for a new two-bedroom, fully furnished apartment overlooking a golf course, or up to £250,000 for a luxury three-bedroom marina apartment with berth for a boat.

Flanking the whole coast are the hills and mountains where towns, villages and countryside are increasingly explored by those seeking rural peace but also nearness to the coast. There is no shortage of farms and houses, either ready to move into, or in need of partial or complete renovation.

Types of property

A typical terraced property in an old part of a town or village is stone-built, possibly with exposed internal beams, windows with shutters on the inside and an iron grille outside, and a pitched roof made of red terracotta tiles. Downstairs there are a living room, kitchen and toilet and upstairs there are a couple of bedrooms and a bathroom. A sun terrace is a bonus, as is a patio at the back.

For those wanting to be closer to the sea, there are towns and villages separated from the long sandy beaches by one-and-a-quarter miles of orange groves. Renovated houses here are in great demand, but so are apartments in new blocks built in recent years to accommodate the steady flow of ex-patriates into the region. Local planning authorities ensure that vast stretches are restricted to low-level housing. These urbanizations often have communal facilities. Buying into an urbanization automatically means becoming a member of the Community of Property Owners. Among other things, the Community ensures the upkeep of the complex and governs the amount of service charges payable. It is worth checking the annual charges, statutes, finances and minutes of AGMs so that you have a full picture before buying.

interesting facts

❖ *El Cid*, the 1961 movie starring Charlton Heston as the eleventh-century hero who drove the Moors from Spain, was filmed in and around Valencia.

❖ Peñíscola was once the residence of Pope Benedict XIII.

❖ Ceramic tile manufacturing, agriculture and tourism are the economic mainstays of the region.

❖ Spain produces 5,127,000 tonnes of citrus fruit per year

What can you get for your money?

These price bands are a guide to the properties you might find.

Under £40,000   small village two-bedroom house needing complete renovation

£50–£75,000   one-bedroom new or resale apartment, off-plan

£75–120,000   two-bedroom luxury apartment, off-plan; or new two-bedroom apartment on golf-course development

£120–180,000   restored three-bedroom farmhouse, in two hectares, 15 kilometres inland; or three-bedroom detached linked villa on golf course; or three-bedroom resale villa, coastal views

£180–250,000   seven-bedroom restored country house, two hectares; or restored inland farmhouse, four bedrooms, pool, gardens

£250,000+   four-bedroom villa, large plot, pool, sea view; or three-bedroom marina apartment with berth for a boat

The inland villages of the Costa del Azahar all have their particular charm, be it location, traditional architecture or historic significance

Points to consider

In some areas and towns, such as Oliva towards the very south of the Costa del Azahar, as many as one in twenty of the local population is British. They often stick together, socialize among themselves and work for each other. They enjoy all the comforts of the UK – TV programmes included – with the added bonus of endless sunshine. There are several international schools dotted along the coast.

budget flights & transport links

FLY TO ALICANTE FROM:
London Luton, London Gatwick (easyJet, Monarch)
London Stansted, Bristol, Liverpool, Newcastle (easyJet)
East Midlands (Bmibaby, easyJet)
Manchester (Bmibaby, Monarch)

FLY TO BARCELONA FROM:
East Midlands (Bmibaby)
Bristol, East Midlands, Liverpool, London Gatwick, London Luton, Newcastle (easyJet)
London Stansted (easyJet, Ryanair)
Dublin, Glasgow (Ryanair)

The Costa del Azahar is served by four international airports (Barcelona, Valencia, Reus and Alicante), and another scheduled at Castelló for 2004. It can also be reached easily by high-speed train, bus and the main A7 coastal motorway. Internally, a car is essential for country living. But many ex-pats living in village communities, with plenty of shops within walking distance, live quite happily without a car and rely on buses for excursions.

House-hunters

Matt Lewis and Nikki Bates

Budget: £70,000

Matt Lewis, a builder, and Nikki Bates, a manager for a mobile phone company, had decided to find a worthwhile way of spending their disposable income. After a number of holidays on the Spanish costas and in the Balearic islands, they came to the Costa del Azahar in search of a holiday home where they would not be surrounded by tourists and could enjoy the laid-back Spanish *mañana*. Matt was hoping to find an older property inland that would have some character, while Nikki favoured white walls, marble floors and sea view. Clearly they would have to reach a compromise.

A luxury two-bedroom penthouse on Oliva beach with two bathrooms, a kitchen, reception room. Two roof terraces. £81,500

A two-bedroom historic townhouse in Oliva with a bathroom, two reception rooms and a kitchen. A large roof terrace, tiny patio and an empty outbuilding. £60,500

Property 1

The first property they saw was a show flat on Oliva beach. The developer had not yet been given planning permission. The living area was open plan with floor-to-ceiling windows giving a view right down to the sea. The pièce de résistance was the vast roof terrace complete with spiral staircase up to another small terrace. Matt felt the property had been well built and tastefully designed with a good use of space, while Nikki could imagine a pool or Jacuzzi on the roof. However, they were nervous about investing their money in the project. The developer did not have a bank guarantee to ensure repayment of any money with interest should anything go wrong. However, he was willing to draw up a private contract to protect the couple's money, although they would have to negotiate the terms and conditions themselves. The positive side was that by buying off-plan the couple would see a 25 per cent appreciation in the value of the property before they even moved in. They decided that, although the show flat was lovely, the twelve- to fourteen-month wait was too long.

Property 2

Next, they travelled inland to the historic town of Oliva, increasingly popular with British buyers, to view a two-bedroom townhouse. The entrance was through a tiled hall used as a study/sitting room, into a fairly basic kitchen. The only bathroom was outside, off the small patio. Upstairs there was a long narrow living room with brick flooring and light flooding in through an end window. The main bedroom had an attractive tiled floor and sturdy wooden shutters. Although renovated, the house needed considerable work to bring it up to scratch. To rewire the whole place would cost between £3,500 and £4,000. The owner was willing to carry out the work before the sale, but Matt and Nikki decided that the property did not have the right feel for them.

Property 3

The Marina Alta mountain range is peppered with tiny villages. Among them, Beniaia is a one-street hamlet with forty houses, several of which have recently been renovated for sale. This 800-year-old house had a dining room with a vaulted ceiling, exposed stonework and an open fire-place. There was a large, well-equipped kitchen lit by a glass brick skylight. The living room also had a vaulted ceiling with polished wooden beams and opened on to a small terrace. The master bedroom was on the second floor with a superb view towards the mountains, while the second bedroom, complete with original Moorish arch, had a separate dressing area and ensuite bathroom. The view from the back terrace was blocked by a wall conforming with regulations that prevent overlooking neighbours' property. However, Matt agreed with the current owner that a raised decking floor would give them the view without invading anybody else's privacy. Overall they felt the house was 'cool, refreshing and quirky', in a close community just an hour's drive from Valencia and Alicante. Only twenty people lived there, with no shops and a restaurant that opened four times a week. Although Matt and Nikki loved the property, the location was wrong for them.

Restored two-bedroom house in the tiny hamlet of Beniaia with two bathrooms, kitchen, two reception rooms. Two terraces. **£73,000**

Property 4

Finally they visited the town of Pego at the foot of the Migdia mountains where an English owner was selling a lovingly restored apartment. The open-plan living area had exposed stone walls, a wooden ceiling, marble kitchen worktops and old-fashioned tiling. The second bedroom was adapted as a dining room while the master bedroom had a balcony with a view right down the town street. The town itself has plenty of bars and restaurants, and is only a twenty-minute drive from Dénia with its regular summer ferries to Ibiza. It was a small property but excellent value for money. The advantage of buying directly from the owner was that there was no estate agent's commission built into the asking price, so they would be saving around £1,500. Matt and Nikki were immediately hooked. 'It looked gorgeous from the outside and we fell in love with everything about it.' Their offer was accepted, and within two weeks they had exchanged contracts and were preparing to enjoy their holiday home.

Historic two-bedroom apartment built into the city walls of Pego. Bathroom, open-plan kitchen and living room. Small balcony. **£50,000**

Ex-pat experience

Gerry and Linda Jack
Oliva, Valencia

When their oldest child reached secondary school age, building contractor Gerry Jack and his wife Linda decided that it was the right moment to fulfil their dream of moving to Spain. Their children were then four, nine and eleven, and went to a local private school where the education was in Spanish. But being thrown in at the deep end worked. They quickly picked up the language and made friends. Luckily, Gerry found work easily when a Spanish friend's cousin took him on with his contracting company. It wasn't long before he was self-employed; four years ago he set up his own limited company with his two sons, by then grown up. Many of their clients are British home-buyers only to happy to find an experienced builder who can speak their language and knows the area.

When they first moved to the Costa del Azahar, there were very few British there but the Jack family made friends through the children's school and Gerry's work. 'I was forty-two when I started learning Spanish. I thought I'd never pick it up, but now I'm not that bad. Of course the children are completely fluent.' Oliva was then a market town on the coast, but there has been a tremendous change in the infrastructure with a lot of new building both in the town and on the outskirts. Old buildings, orange groves and country roads have disappeared as popular new apartment blocks sprang up complete with new offices and shops close to the beach.

'Integrate with the Spaniards and learn colloquial Spanish. Without it, you're lost.'

'If you move with children, do it when they're young. They can pick up a language and integrate quickly.'

Moving in their forties did have its problems. 'It can take several attempts to get things done. It's not the way I was brought up, where the client gets what he wants when he asks for it. You have to get used to a different way of life, and working in such a hot climate takes some getting used to.' The Jacks found the paperwork applying for residency was difficult, although that has changed now thanks to the EU. Similarly the tax laws can be complicated, so Gerry views integrating with the Spanish, learning the language and getting legal advice as essential, so that you can get on with your life and enjoy it.

After fourteen years, the Jack family love their life. 'People are laid back. Everything is done *mañana* and the family always comes first in everyone's list of priorities.' They have never been back to England since they left. They remain in touch with friends by telephone, and the most recent addition to the household is Linda's eighty-two-year-old mother who couldn't resist joining them at last.

How to buy a property in Spain

A general guide

It is recommended that you take professional advice to check the contracts you are signing. It is also important to decide in whose name the deed should be registered, because of the inheritance implications, and whether or not to make a Spanish will.

Why you need a solicitor or *gestor*

Each sale varies in its detail. You may want to employ the services of a specialist English solicitor, a Spanish lawyer, or a *gestor*, a licensed professional who, for a reasonable fee, will act as the middleman between you and the Spanish bureaucracy. A *gestor* is not a solicitor but can handle your paperwork for the purchase of a property, your taxes, setting up a business and more. Your *gestor* or your solicitor will conduct searches to ensure various aspects of the purchase are going as planned: checking that you are buying what you think you are buying in terms of the property and surrounding land; checking that the seller has legal title to the property; checking that there are no unpaid debts accrued against the property; ascertaining if there are any building restrictions imposed by the local authority and so on.

Exchanging contracts

Generally, when you have chosen your property, a private contract (*contrato privado de compraventa*) is drawn up which specifies details of the buyer and seller, purchase price, deposit (usually 10 per cent), completion date, method of payment, any extras you have agreed to buy and any other relevant terms or conditions. This is a binding contract and your deposit can be refunded only under certain strict conditions. Make sure you understand what these are. It is common practice for the sale and purchase price to be understated so that the seller's liability for capital gains tax is reduced. Remember, when you come to sell and the actual price is declared, you will be liable to pay the tax on the additional profit.

Buying off-plan

If you are buying 'off-plan' – that is, the property is still being built – payments will be made in agreed stages that vary according to the developer. You, or your representative, must check the work is completed satisfactorily at each stage. Make sure the contract allows you to get a bank guarantee covering you against the risk of the seller going bust before finishing the project, and to retain a final payment until six to twelve months after the building is finished so you can recall the builder if there are any faults.

Completing the contract

The purchase is usually completed up to three or four months later in front of the notary (*notario*) when the final deed (*escritura de compraventa*) is signed by you or someone you have invested with power of attorney. Property is sold in the condition in which it is at the time of completion, so it should be checked by you and/or your representative. At this point the balance of the money is due and the keys will be handed over. After signing, your lawyer will pay the taxes due and lodge the deed with the land registry to register the change in title formally. This may take three months or more, by which time land registry fees are due. The *gestor* should give you a copy of the deed so that your lawyer can complete the other legal formalities.

Registration

The registration is vital. Even when you have signed the contract, charges can be registered against the property without your knowledge until the property is registered in your name.

Additional fees

The notary's fees are set by the government and are due after completion. You should budget approximately 10 per cent of the purchase price to cover the additional taxes, Land Registry fees, notary fees and legal fees, not forgetting the cost of insuring the property.

Countryside

'The country habit has me by the heart,
For he's bewitched for ever who has seen,
Not with his eyes but with his vision, Spring
Flow down the woods and stipple leaves with sun.'
Vita Sackville-West, 'Winter', *The Land*, **1926**

Creuse

Limousin, France

La Celle Dunoise is one of the most attractive villages on the banks of the River Creuse

websites

www.cg23.fr
the department's official guide

www.lacreuse.com
introduction to the region

www.houseofceramicsfrance.com
for French classes for ex-pats in northern Creuse

Despite being roughly the same size as Wales, fewer than 150,000 people live in Creuse, making it one of the least densely populated parts of Europe – it is even said that there are more Limousin cows there than people. The landscape is lush and green with a quarter of it covered by dense forest. It sits on the north-western fringes of the Massif Central and drops down through the undulating landscape towards the Creuse river valley. In the nineteenth century, it was thought to be such a perfect example of the French countryside that the Ecole de Crozant was born, composed of landscape painters, including Claude Monet, who flocked to the region inspired by the scenery along the Creuse river. Creuse, Haute-Vienne and Corrèze are the three departments that make up the Limousin region. One of the most rural departments of France, Creuse remains remarkably unspoilt with only two major roads cutting through it and very little development.

Like everywhere else in France, the inhabitants of Limousin take great pride in their cuisine. Specialities include the Limousin beef, chestnuts, wild mushrooms and *foie gras*, *clafoutis* (black cherry pudding) and local cheese.

Where to go

This is a sleepy part of the world where the tourist highlight in the principal town of **Guéret** is the Musée de la Sénatorerie, with its collection of enamels and ceramics, while just outside the town is a giant maze-cum-adventure park. The attractive market town of **Aubusson** is synonymous with the carpets and tapestries made there. It sits on the banks of the River Creuse whose water was crucial to the making of wool dyes and washing the wool. Every August, Aubusson hosts the world's largest cheese market. To the south is **Felletin**, also famous for its weaving but known too as the gateway to the Plateau Millevaches (plain of a thousand springs) that extends into neighbouring Corrèze and is the source of the rivers Creuse, Vienne, Corrèze and Vézère.

Throughout the region are small farming hamlets, historic villages and towns where life is unhurried and undisturbed. In the north-east of the department, the well-preserved medieval streets of the fortified town of **Boussac** focus on its twelfth-century castle where the novelist George Sand lived and set her first novel, *Jeanne*. To the west is the busy market town of **La Souterraine**, one of the stopping points on the pilgrims' route to Santiago de Compostela. **Bourganeuf** was once a wealthy medieval town used by the Knights Templar, but has become known more recently for being the first place in France to get electricity. **Evaux-les-Bains** is the only spa town in Limousin, whose thermal waters have benefited sufferers since Roman times.

Watersports enthusiasts will be satisfied higher up the Grande Creuse river where Le Pays des Trois Lacs provides opportunities for fishing, bathing and other pursuits, or by going to Lac de Vassivière on the border with Corrèze.

Creuse may seem remote but it is only a short drive from the attractions of the other two departments of Limousin. The regional capital is **Limoges**, famed throughout the world for its porcelain and enamel. The city itself is steeped in history, having been founded in 16 BC by the Roman Emperor Augustus. Through its turbulent history Limoges has been razed to the ground and rebuilt no fewer than five times. Many granite and half-timbered buildings are still standing in the old quarter, many of them recently restored. Although Creuse has plenty of attractive historical villages, none has yet been given the coveted 'Most Beautiful Villages of France' award. However, a short trip to Corrèze leads to six such villages: **Collonges-la-Rouge**, with its brilliant red sandstone turreted buildings; **Turenne**, huddled in the shadow of its castle; Curemont, with its three châteaux; the half-timbered houses of **Ségur-le-Chateau**; the medieval town of **Saint Robert**; and **Treignac** on the Vézère river.

highlights

❋ The ancient city of Limoges
❋ Musée Départmental de la Tapisserie in Aubusson
❋ Musée de la Sénatorerie in Guéret
❋ Exploring the historic villages
❋ Relishing the countryside and what it offers

weather

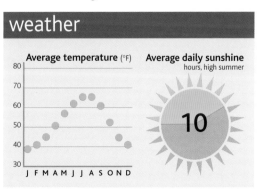

Average temperature (°F)

Average daily sunshine
hours, high summer

10

J F M A M J J A S O N D

The village of Crozant lies where the Petite Creuse River meets the Grande Creuse. The surrounding landscape has inspired an entire school of painting

Property

For years, stonemasonry was one of the mainstays of the Creusois economy. Until the mid-nineteenth century, Creusois stonemasons would walk for the best part of a week to find work in Paris. Their skills were in demand all over France, where they were responsible for building numerous châteaux or *maisons bourgeoises*. Thanks to subsequent migration away from this already sparsely populated countryside to towns and cities, there are many old houses, some of them derelict, to be found here.

Types of property

Typical Creuse country houses usually have thick (almost one metre) granite walls with black slate roofs, and often have a converted *grenier* or loft. Internally, they may have exposed oak or chestnut beams, flagstone floors and open granite fireplaces. If you are lucky, you will find Creusois cobbled floors and a bread oven. Grander houses have marble fireplaces in several rooms, oak floors and panelling. Externally, character is added with heavy sills and lintels, sometimes with decorative carvings. The houses often have shutters and some have tiny windows beneath the guttering from the days when the grain stored in the loft needed ventilation. Former farmhouses are usually in a small hamlet and frequently have a barn attached into which they can be extended. Many stone village houses have gardens that are separate from the property, sometimes across a road. This often makes them harder to sell and, as a result, a little cheaper.

What can you get for your money?

These price bands are a guide to the properties you might find.

£10–15,000	**small farmhouse, in need of complete restoration, with outbuilding, small garden; or small derelict town or village house**
£15–30,000	**basic but habitable traditional country or townhouse, three or four bedrooms, sanitation, but may need new kitchen and bathroom**
£30–50,000	**farmhouse with outbuildings, 2,000 square metres of land; or converted hamlet house with large garden; or townhouse, six bedrooms, garage, needing some work**
£50–70,000	**large farmhouse (possibly two adjoining, one for conversion into a *gîte*), outbuildings, land; or excellent townhouse, good kitchen and garden**

£70–100,000	well-kept renovated farm, central heating, double-glazing etc., large garden and land; or townhouse with courtyard and view in better town
£100–150,000	farmhouse in excellent condition, numerous outbuildings, 4,000 square metres of land; or top-of-the-range town or village house with large garden
£150–200,000	small country 'hamlet' with *gîtes*, barns, workshops, one hectare of land; or townhouse, five/six bedrooms, very large reception rooms, original features
£200–250,000	small château being run as B&B
£250,000+	large immaculate farm, several hectares of land, other habitable houses, barns, etc.

interesting facts

* Novelist George Sand and her composer lover Frédéric Chopin spent many happy summers in northern Creuse.

* Weavers from Felletin in southern Creuse made Graham Sutherland's tapestry in Coventry Cathedral.

* Impressionist Claude Monet, inspired by the local countryside, painted many pictures here

The roof tops of a typical Creusois town

Points to consider

There are reports of property price rises of almost 25 per cent within a year, but there are still plenty of bargains to be found. Budgets stretch much further than in other areas to which the British have gravitated in recent years, such as Provence and the Dordogne. The whole area is becoming popular with ex-pats, especially the Dutch and now the British. Although this is quintessential rural France, many choose to live either in or within walking distance of hamlets and villages with their bars and shops. The British who move to Creuse tend to integrate with the locals. Little English is spoken, and a good working knowledge of French is essential. However, three areas are popular: the flattish countryside around the pretty town of La Souterraine in the north-west; the three man-made lakes north of Guéret (population: 130,100); and the hilly forests in the south near Aubusson, and Lac de Vassivière.

budget flights & transport links

FLY TO LIMOGES AND POITIERS FROM:
London Stansted (Ryanair)

There are railway links from Paris to Limoges or Châteauroux while the region is about six hours by motorway from Calais to Guéret. A car is essential in Creuse (there are buses for schoolchildren and old folk). Roads are good, windy but quiet.

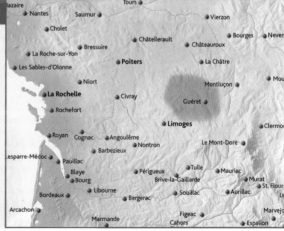

House-hunters

Paul Dennis and Lita Phillips
Budget: £24,000

Four-bedroom traditional village house near La Souterraine with living room, kitchen and bathroom. **£20,000**

Two-bedroom country cottage near Boussac with a living/dining room, kitchen and bathroom, 1,000 square metres of land. **£24,000**

A love of rural life led carpenter Paul Dennis and his partner Lita Phillips to Creuse. 'It is relatively undiscovered, the prices low and the countryside incomparable.' They are planning to live the good life, with enough outside space to grow vegetables and keep chickens, ducks and maybe even a pig.

Property 1

In one of the villages surrounding La Souterraine was a traditional house built out of local granite 100 years ago. It was decorated throughout in busy patterned wallpaper which, though very French, was something Lita felt would have to go. Paul is the chef of the couple and liked the kitchen but felt it was on the small side. The bedrooms had working fireplaces and Paul and Lita thought they might convert the downstairs into a larger kitchen. The property had been on the market for a year, largely because it had no land attached. However, there was a 200-year-old barn in front of the house that sat on 2,000 square metres of land. The same vendors had the barn and land on the market separately for £13,000 but were prepared to sell the two lots together for £30,000. The couple liked the 'very typically French rustic' property, 'but we do want a garden, so it has to be no'.

Property 2

The next property they saw was a 150-year-old stone cottage near Boussac. The living room felt very French with its tiled floor and heavy original beams. The country kitchen was very light although it needed some structural alterations.

The main bedroom was big enough to fit in the four-poster bed that Paul had made for Lita. Outside there was a big garden and a pigsty that could be restored ready for their proposed pig or turned into a workshop for Paul. Originally the lower floor of the house would have been used for living quarters while the upstairs would have been used for storage, hence the stone steps up the side of the house. The property was not being sold with furniture but the price did include the wood-burner in the living room. To install central heating would cost about £5,000. Paul and Lita were delighted with the property. 'We both loved it although it was perhaps a little too small for our needs.'

Property 3

Nonetheless they went on to see two further properties. The first was near Bourganeuf. Here two farmhouses offered Paul and Lita a real opportunity for getting their hands dirty in return for their dream home. Between the two buildings, there were all the features of a working farm but neither of the houses had electricity, plumbing, insulation or heating although structurally they were perfectly sound with roofs in good condition. The renovation of the main house would cost an estimated £15,000. A natural spring provided a constant supply of crystal clear water to the farmyard. For £50, they could have it tested by a state laboratory to see if it was suitable for drinking. 'It's amazing for the money. We love it.'

Three-bedroom farmhouse in need of restoration with kitchen/dining room and large loft. Second farmhouse with cowshed, pigsty and 1,000 square metres of land. £29,000

Property 4

The last property they saw was in a small hamlet outside Aubusson where a barn had been converted into an interesting living space. The living room was spacious with exposed beams and a large fireplace. The compact kitchen allowed a small dining area while the master bedroom in the loft space was big enough to have an end closed off as a shower room. The garden was large enough to be divided so that, as well as having vegetables and livestock, Paul and Lita would be able to entertain out there. The owner had renovated it over eight years as a real labour of love, spending £4,000 on a new roof and another £6,000 on tiles, stairs, kitchen and bathroom. It was in an idyllic situation with a strong community spirit in the hamlet, but Paul and Lita were put off because there was no land directly attached to it.

Their minds were made up. They offered the asking price on the third property they saw and their offer was accepted. Within a month they'd sold their Worcestershire home and on 10 November 2002 they signed the contract. 'Now we're here, it's just as wonderful as when we first saw it. We are building the dream! We expected to have problems but there hasn't been anything we couldn't get over. It has been difficult getting the essential workmen, such as electricians, when we need them. We weren't allowed a building permit for a septic tank but fortunately we also own land over the road where we can put a sand filter system instead. The *Mairie* has been exceptional and has helped us with all the paperwork where our French would have let us down.' As their project comes together stage by stage, Paul and Lita are looking forward to moving out of their rented accommodation and into their new home. When work on the main house is finished, they plan to renovate the second house as a rural *gîte* to provide a small income.

Renovated nineteenth-century barn outside Aubusson with two bedrooms, kitchen, living/dining room, bathroom, 1,000 square metres of land. £19,000

Ex-pat experience

Steve and Sylvia Sales
Cressat, Creuse

Susan and John Sales with their daughter, Catherine

Owning a smallholding in Worcestershire was the ideal preparation for Steve and Sylvia Sales' eventual move to France. Tired of the two-hour commute to Birmingham and the worsening traffic, they decided to give up their respective jobs in medicine and dental research and buy a larger farm. Unable to afford anything in the UK, they saw an ad in *Farmer's Weekly* for a property near Guéret. 'We didn't really intend to buy but met up with the agent who showed us several. No one had lived here for four years. There were two big stone barns, a pigsty that's now a *gîte*, a farmer's house for us, the principal house used as a workshop, a small stable block and 250 acres.' The deal took some time to go through because the sale of any farmland in France has to go through SAFER (Société d'Aménagement Foncier et d'Etablissement Rural), which has a first option to purchase farmland.

Their neighbours regarded them with interest and were ready to help as Sylvia set up their herd of Limousin cattle. 'It is unusual being a woman farmer here and rarer still an English one. And there's a lot more to learn than looking after cows. The difficult thing is the bureaucracy but a neighbouring farmer taught me the scope of the necessary paperwork and where to go to get things. He also helped me join a co-operative for major investments such as a tractor and plough.'

'If moving to France permanently, do some sort of work involving French people.'

The couple settled easily into the local community. 'It didn't feel as if it took long since we had to get things up and running so fast we were concentrating on that. The French like and understand it if you are trying to do something.' In the first instance they made friends through farming until, in 1996, they had a baby, Catherine, which inevitably involved Sylvia with other mothers and children. 'If you have children it makes a difference too and cements your relationship with the community more.' They have also been incredibly fortunate to have two elderly neighbours who dote on Catherine. 'She goes there every day after school. She's like their grandchild. They have never ever been ill nor said they can't have her or even let us pay them.'

'Never upset anyone for the first five years. Everyone seems to be related and you can't foresee the repercussions.'

Catherine is fluent in French, speaking it with her French 'grandparents' and at school while her English, used only at home, is slightly less good.

The nearby town of Jarnages has everything they need, from a school to two supermarkets, although plenty of fresh produce can be got direct from the local farms. They miss their friends and having culture on their doorstep but they do have lots of space, little traffic and are part of a community that rallies round when needed. After ten years, the farm is flourishing, the *gîte* is up and running (http://family.sales.chez.tiscali.fr/) and the gamble the Saleses took is more than paying off.

La Rioja

Northern Spain

La Rioja, Spain's smallest autonomous region, has taken its place on the world stage as the country's leading producer of fine wines. Cut off from the Basque region and Navarre by the Ebro river flowing along its northern boundary and by dramatic sierras from the regions of Soria and Burgos to the south and west, La Rioja is divided into two: the Rioja Alta and the Rioja Baja. The Rioja Alta is the more mountainous area to the west of the capital Logroño, renowned for its vineyards and wine. To the east of the capital lies the Rioja Baja, with the fertile plains of the Ebro valley given over to growing vegetables of all kinds but particularly asparagus, artichokes, tomatoes and red peppers.

The region has had more than its fair share of rulers. Since the Romans, invading Germanic tribes and the Moors took successive control, it has also been the subject of disputes between Navarre, Castille and Aragón. Only in 1982 did La Rioja become an autonomous community.

The west of La Rioja is characterised by the stretches of vineyards that produce Spain's best-known wine

The Riojans are as proud of their local cuisine as they are of their wine. Specialities include *patatas a la riojana* (potatoes and chorizo), *pimientos rellanos de merluza* (peppers stuffed with cod brandade), *calcots y esparragus con romesco* (lamb and asparagus), rich meat stews from the mountains and roast lamb. Vegetables are used generously. There are weekly markets throughout the region.

websites

www.spanish-living.com for general information on living in Spain, including property and law

www.cmrioja.es for the General Directorate of Industry, Tourism, Labour and Commerce; exhaustive information on La Rioja

Where to go

The principal town is **Logroño**, founded by the Romans and built on the River Ebro. It came into its own once a stone bridge was built across the river, making the town an important staging post for medieval pilgrims journeying along the Camino de Santiago from France to Santiago de Compostela. Now a thriving modern town, its old quarter hugs the river bank but centres on its gothic cathedral and the Iglesia de Santiago el Real. Local tradition continues with the Fiesta de Vendimia Riojana in September, a week-long celebration of the grape harvest that includes treading and blessing the grapes.

To the west, there are several historic towns and villages that sprang up round the monasteries built on the pilgrims' route, including **Nájera**, the capital of La Rioja and Navarra until the eleventh century; **Santo Domingo de Calzada**; and **San Millán de la Cogolla** with the monasteries of San Millán de Suso on the mountainside and San Millán de Yuso in the lush Cárdenas valley. The lively town of **Haro**, situated on a hill at the mouth of the Tirón river, is at the centre of the Riojan wine country. Here cobbled alleyways are packed with bars and vintners among several palaces and mansions built by prosperous wine merchants. Every June it celebrates the Fiesta de San Felices which climaxes in the Batalla del Vino, a Bacchanalian riot of wine-throwing.

Surrounded by orchards and fields of vegetables, **Calahorra** is the main market town in the Rioja Baja. Of Roman origins, the town overlooks the fertile Cidacos plains and makes a good starting point for exploring the rest of the region, famous for its 5,000 dinosaur footprints. The Riojan countryside is dotted with attractive historic towns and villages, among them **Arnedillo**, known for its thermal springs; **Enciso**, site of the biggest group of dinosaur prints; and **Anguiano**, which comes to life every July and September with the traditional Danza de los Zancos, when stilt dancers spin through the steep streets.

The different landscapes of La Rioja afford endless possibilities for outdoor pursuits whether winter sports in the ski resort of Valdezcaray in the west, watersports in the González Lacasa dam near El Rasillo or down the Iregua and Najerilla rivers, fishing in the Ebro and its tributaries, hiking, climbing or mountain biking. Only an hour and a half's drive from the northern coast, La Rioja is a region of stunning beauty unspoilt by tourism and largely undiscovered by the British home-buyer.

highlights

❋ The Camino de Santiago

❋ Dinosaur footprints in the Rioja Baja

❋ Wine tasting in the *bodegas* of Haro

❋ The medieval hill-top town of Briones

❋ UNESCO heritage site of San Millán Yuso and Suso Monasteries

weather

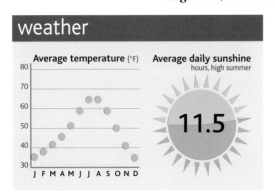

Average temperature (°F)

Average daily sunshine
hours, high summer

11.5

J F M A M J J A S O N D

Property

Nine out of ten of La Rioja's 260,000 inhabitants now live in one of its ten major towns, and half of those live in the capital Logroño. There is also a thriving ex-pat community of professionals and their families (more French than British), where several multinationals such as Electrolux and Schweppes have factories. However, this does not automatically mean rich pickings for house-hunters in abandoned rural villages. La Rioja is one of a handful of Spanish regions that enjoy a higher standard of living than not only the rest of the country but also higher than the European average. This is reflected in buoyant property prices.

The mountains of Rioja hide plenty of villages ideal for a remote retreat

The urban worker's prosperity often allows him to retain the old family home in the village as a weekend and holiday retreat.

The introduction of the euro resulted in a surge of property prices throughout Spain, since anyone with pesetas derived from the black economy hurriedly invested them in bricks and mortar before they became valueless. La Rioja is no exception, and prices have allegedly risen by as much as 50–300 per cent in the past five years, depending on the location. However, property prices, although high for Spain, are not as expensive as those in neighbouring Navarre and the Basque country to the north.

Types of property

Some of the more desirable properties in La Rioja Alta are the *casas blasonadas*, which rarely come on the market. Often they are passed on to friends or kept in the family because grants can be obtained for repairs. They are grand, three- or four-storey, seventeenth- and eighteenth-century balconied village houses that bear a family coat of arms. The second-home market in this part of La Rioja tends to be limited to Spaniards who buy into modern developments of apartments with sports facilities outside the towns, though village houses and *fincas* can be found for the more adventurous home-buyers.

The few foreign buyers in La Rioja Baja have tended to buy farmhouses on rural sites. These may be old stone properties with tiled roofs, new properties with rendered walls or a combination of both. The traditional farmhouses have six to eight rooms on the upper floor with a kitchen and living room, previously the barn or stable, downstairs and no sanitation.

interesting facts

❋ La Rioja is the administrative 'autonomous community' but Rioja (without 'La') refers to the wider wine-producing area.

❋ 300 million bottles and 25 different varieties of Riojan wine are produced each year.

❋ Riojan wines were first officially documented back in 1102.

❋ The village church in Manzanares chimes like Big Ben.

❋ The cockle shell was the emblem of the pilgrims.

What can you get for your money?

These price bands are a guide to the properties you might find.

£15–20,000	small building site, land only
£20–35,000	remote mountain village house, unmodernized, 75–200 square metres
£35–45,000	better village house, near Logroño
£60–100,000	three-/four-bedroom flat, 60–75 square metres, needing some modernization
£65–130,000	renovated village house
£120–160,000	new flats/apartments in Logroño; or new semi-detached village house, garden, perhaps pool
£160–200,000	new semi-detached house, small garden and communal facilities (pool, etc.) in or near Logroño
£200–270,000	new detached house with communal facilities in or near Logroño
£235,000+	detached house in or near Logroño with large garden, pool

Calahorra is a farming and manufacturing centre lying on the plains of the River Ebro

Points to consider

It is difficult to buy plots of building land outside certain zones close to the towns unless there is an existing farmhouse or building there. Mountain villages in the valleys running north towards the River Ebro, may be an attractive prospect in the summer, but not so appealing in the depth of winter. They can be cut off by snow for days on end. Houses here are often second homes, used mainly in the summer months, either by locals or outsiders. In Valdezcaray, the ski resort, the houses more closely resemble those in the French Pyrenees with wide sloping slate roofs and wooden shutters.

budget flights & transport links

FLY TO BILBAO FROM:
London Gatwick (British Airways)
London Stansted (easyJet)

Ferries run from the UK to Santander or Bilbao. Local and intercity bus services are good and cheap. Rail services are improving with high-speed trains to Madrid and Barcelona,

both via Zaragoza. The Bilbao–Barcelona motorway runs along the Ebro corridor at the northern border of La Rioja. The region is crossed by dual carriageway/trunk links with Pamplona, Vitoria, Burgos and Soria (each about an hour from Logroño).

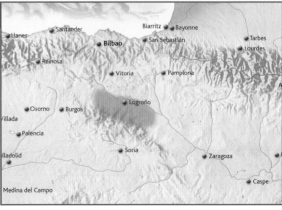

House-hunters

Peter and Denise Scott
Budget: £60,000

A passion for gardening and a love of the Spanish way of life took Peter and Denise Scott to Rioja in search of a holiday home where the mild winters and rich soil make it a gardener's paradise. They were looking for a house with character plus a garden and two bedrooms so they could invite friends and family to stay.

Property 1

Their first port of call was just across the border with Aragón in the historic town of Tarazona. Founded around 300 BC, the mix of 2,500 years of architecture is reflected in the city's skyline. With a population of 11,000, the town has plenty of shops, bars and restaurants. A unique house built into the city's medieval walls was on the market. The living room was very light with astounding views across the rooftops, taking in the cathedral, bishop's palace and the bullring, and the all-white kitchen had a contemporary luxury feel. The master bedroom was large with different ceiling heights and had an attractive skylight. On the lower floor was a surprise bar area with masses of room for entertaining. The house was originally built in the sixteenth century but was renovated to a very high standard in 2002. Being in a protected area, the façade of the building must remain untouched, while the regulation prohibiting buildings from being over two storeys high meant the property's uninterrupted views would be secure.

Two-bedroom historic house in Tarazona with living room, kitchen/dining room, bathroom and large downstairs bar area. Roof terrace. **£74,000**

Property 2

Next they headed to the Moncayo National Park in the south-east of La Rioja. After five years waiting for planning permission, a small development of villas had been built in superb surroundings. Two large living room windows meant the room was beautifully light and benefited from the superb views while the L-shaped kitchen had all the essentials with room for a small dining area. One bedroom had fitted cupboards with room for a single bed and a double sofabed while the other was situated on an open mezzanine floor looking down to the living area. The villa had a small front garden and a much larger unplanted one at the back where Peter could envisage growing peach trees. It can be dry in the summer months so it would be worth considering installing an irrigation system for around £300. 'It's a very pleasant little house with marvellous terrace views. The garden would keep Peter busy for a long time.' The development was very quiet,

Two-bedroom villa in the Moncayo National Park with living/dining room, kitchen and bathroom. Terrace. Access to communal pool and other sports facilities. **£58,000**

divided equally between holiday and residential homes, and benefiting from a communal pool, tennis, squash and basketball courts, a games room and bar. Although Peter and Denise thought the setting was out of this world, they felt the villa lacked the authentic Spanish character that they were hoping to find.

Property 3

Pradillo is an unspoilt mountain village ten minutes outside Logroño. There, an unusual house with a tower crowned with a roof terrace had been renovated two years earlier. The entrance still boasted the original fourteenth-century wooden door, restored by a local craftsman. Inside there was a large L-shaped living room with a tiled floor, a newly fitted kitchen with brand new appliances included in the price, three bedrooms with views of the village and a new bathroom decorated with locally made blue and white tiles. The terrace at the top of the tower was shaded by its roof but a sunnier terrace could be created by building across the bedroom roofs at an estimated cost of £2,500. Peter and Denise loved the location. 'Round every village corner is more beautiful than the last. The house is stunning and we could move in immediately.' Pradillo welcomes 3,500 tourists during the summer so it was interesting to learn that the house could be rented for £250 a week. Ultimately, however, they felt that the property needed the attention of someone who was going to live there full-time. Although they loved the house, the downside was there was no garden and Peter would not be happy without his outside space.

Recently renovated three-bedroom village house in Pradillo with living room, kitchen, bathroom and shower room. Tower with roof terrace.

£55,500

Property 4

The last property they saw was in the country just minutes from Haro. It was a substantial house that had had little done to it over the years but it had enormous potential. The living rooms were small and rather dingy but the two storerooms had fantastic potential to transform the house. The underhouse storage had once been used for the owner's animals – the pens were still there. It had also been used as the village dance hall and was the centre of the village in days gone by. The two possibilities were to either extend, making them part of the main house, or to make a separate unit of them that might be rented out. Either way, the cost of the work would amount to £24,000. Outside, the garden offered as much potential again. The owner assured them that the vine produced enough grapes for two bottles of wine. Peter and Denise's eyes lit up when they heard there was room to plant another 120. However, ultimately, it was more of a project than they wanted to take on.

Three-bedroom rural property near Haro with three reception rooms, a kitchen, bathroom, cellar and store rooms. Large mature garden and garage.

£63,000

Torn between the first and third properties, Peter and Denise made some further enquiries. They did revisit the house in Pradillo but decided that it was too remote for them. Undaunted by their lack of success first time round, they hope to return to La Rioja to look again, but are also exploring other areas in southern Spain.

Ex-pat experience

Ian Thomas
Logroño, La Rioja

Driving across the border from France into the Basque country was enough for Ian Thomas to fall in love with northern Spain. Working in a language school in Catalonia led him to want to set up one of his own. After he'd looked around the various regions, he settled on La Rioja where the economy was waking up, making it a good time to start a business. Since moving there Ian has seen the agriculturally based economy change with the influx of industry into Logroño where he now lives. He found it easy to integrate and make friends. 'The Spaniards are very hospitable, I could speak the language and by chance found a group of drinking friends. There are plenty of evening classes through which one could meet people although I have only gone on wine-tasting courses, wine being my big interest.' As for culture, there is plenty to do, including a local theatre, amateur dramatic groups, concerts and two cinema complexes.

> 'The climate has the best of both Atlantic and Mediterranean influences and our quality of life just keeps on improving.'

He and his Spanish wife, Charo, have moved from an apartment to a semi-detached chalet in a totally enclosed estate of 50 houses on the banks of the Ebro, near the centre of town. The community has a village-like atmosphere although it is extremely cosmopolitan with neighbours from France, Germany and Morocco. They have an open-air communal pool but in the winter can use the pool in the sports centre next door. Although they are on good terms with a number of British acquaintances, the Thomases do not make a point of socializing with the English community out here. 'We have a small and "exclusive" group of close friends and of course all of Charo's family is here too.' One and a half years ago, they adopted Alba Ning, their Chinese daughter who is now three and growing up to speak both Spanish and English. When she is four, she will go to the local Spanish school where she will receive a bilingual education with some French as well until she is eighteen. Ian has no reservations whatsoever when it comes to either the Spanish education or healthcare systems.

Ian Thomas with his daughter Alba Ning

Ian and Charo now run a language consultancy together. The normal working day runs from 9 a.m. to 2 p.m. and then 4.30 p.m. until 8 p.m., with time to go home for lunch in the middle. At the height of the summer they work a more intensive day, running from 8 a.m. until 2 p.m. when they can go home comfortable in the knowledge that other businesses have shut down too.

Despite having lived in Spain for over twenty years, Ian still misses being able to watch cricket and rugby although he has hopes of connecting to digital TV soon. Otherwise he has few complaints about life in La Rioja. 'The only things I would like is to see fewer Irish-themed pubs, more variety in restaurant cuisine and to be nearer than a one and a half hours' drive from the beach. Apart from that I can't complain.'

Charente

Poitou-Charentes, France

Old merchants' houses stand on the banks of the River Charente in Saint-Sauvignon

A rolling landscape of vast fields of sunflowers stretching into the distance, sleepy historic villages surrounded by vineyards, small châteaux built by wealthy cognac producers and the slow-flowing River Charente – just a few of the pleasures in store in the French department of Charente. One of the four departments of Poitou-Charentes, it follows the river valley as it meanders from Angoulême to the Atlantic coast. Called 'the most beautiful stream in my kingdom' by François I of France, it has been the region's lifeline for centuries. From Roman days onwards, it served as an important trade route used to transport salt, brandy and armaments to the coast. Today it is used almost exclusively for pleasure, with opportunities for swimming, fishing and messing about in boats. In the foothills of the Massif Central are two man-made mountain lakes – the lacs Lavaud and Mas Chaban – where white sands and clean mountain spring water lie in the shade of oak and chestnut trees. Watersports, golf, horse-riding trails and walking are among the attractions here.

Apart from brandy, the region is known for *pineau* – a fortified aperitif made from a blend of unfermented grape juice and brandy – and for its wines. The Limousin cattle seen grazing over the region produce other specialities of butter and beef, while the lamb from Confolens is known for its quality.

Where to go

The principal town of the area is **Angoulême**, known for its paper mills, most of which have now shut down. Its situation on a plateau overlooking the river provided a natural defence when it was fought over in the Anglo-French wars and the later Wars of Religion. Its focus is the Place Laval, where the Hôtel de Ville stands on the site of the palace of the ducs d'Angoulême; the surrounding maze of streets have been largely restored and pedestrianized. The town's other main attractions are its Cathédral St Pierre and the Centre National de Bande Dessinée

et de l'Image (comic strip museum). A few miles east is the charming medieval town of Confolens with its ancient stone bridge and its renowned folk festival that brings the town to life every August.

Downstream is the intoxicating town of **Cognac**, where lichen-stained buildings and a certain something in the air (known as 'the angels' share') betray the presence of its main product. Once a salt-producing town, Cognac is now synonymous with its brandy. Not only the *eau de vie* itself but the corks and bottles are produced here too. The picturesque medieval streets of half-timbered and stone houses rub shoulders with the castle where François I was born.

Saintes was once the capital of the Saintonge province and as such is an important town in the history of Aquitaine. Its historical centre is well preserved and the town also boasts a Gallo-Roman amphitheatre, the arch that marked the bridge built for pilgrims travelling across the river to Santiago de Compostela, and two pilgrim churches. There are a number of castles and Romanesque churches in the surrounding countryside and, of course, small towns and villages all with their own history and architecture. Among them are **Aubeterre-sur-Dronne**, hailed as one of the most beautiful villages in France; **Tusson**, with medieval and Renaissance buildings protected by a preservation order; and **La Rochefoucauld**, overlooked by its immense Renaissance château.

The people of Charente are said to live at the speed that cognac ages, so renowned is their relaxed attitude to life. They claim some of the best weather in France, saying winters only last three weeks.

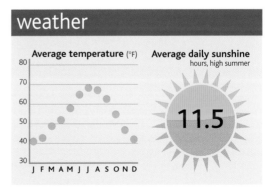

weather

Average temperature (°F)

Average daily sunshine
hours, high summer

11.5

J F M A M J J A S O N D

A stone gateway frames the leafy façade of a house near Cognac

Property

Prices have risen at least 10 per cent each year since the millennium and are still on the up. The region is peppered with charming towns, pretty hamlets and farmhouses. Prices are high along the sandy beaches of Charente-Maritime but the further inland you go, the greater the bargains to be found. Foreign buyers tend to be British but there are also Belgians, Swiss and Americans. The British gravitate towards the hillier and more wooded countryside in the north-east of the department, especially around the small town of Confolens.

Types of property

Charente has an extraordinary choice of property to suit almost any pocket. There are tumbledown barns and impressive châteaux, and everything in between, including country homes – with spacious internal courtyards and impressive entrances, superb fireplaces and enormous outbuildings. Limestone village houses are often built in a U-shape with the living area in the centre and the bedrooms in either side. They frequently have porches with pretty relief mouldings, gardens and outbuildings at the back. Generally Charente has retained a traditional feel; while modern buildings can be found, they are usually bungalow-style and in the suburbs. In Confolens, reasonably priced countryside plots are available as well as properties ranging from a renovated one-bedroom village house or a group of three run-down buildings ripe for renovation, to much more elaborate country homes.

Possibly the most difficult property to find, because they are the most popular and are often snapped up before going on the open market, is what is known as a *charentaise*, often selling at roughly £150,000. This is an eighteenth- or nineteenth-century country house, forming one side of a courtyard, with other sides being either a building (possibly converted into living accommodation) or walls. Built of local limestone (almost peach-coloured when dressed), the main building is frequently approached through arched gates, and has four rooms both upstairs and downstairs, with tall shuttered windows. The most desirable have red terracotta-tile roofs. The town equivalent is a *maison bourgeoise*, a tall and elegant three-storey house with a slate roof. A *charentaise* often retains original features such as a stone sink, situated near the entrance, and with a bull's eye window above it. If you are lucky, an outbuilding may have a bread oven and a stable building with a patterned cobbled floor.

interesting facts

❋ Saintes is the birthplace of Dr Guillotin, who advocated execution by decapitation.

❋ La Charente was 'France's happiest river', according to the French King Henry IV.

❋ You can view desirable properties from a cruise boat on the Charente river.

❋ The huge blues skies of Charente attract artists from all over the world.

What can you get for your money?

These price bands are a guide to the properties you might find.

£15–25,000	sizeable building land in good location; or habitable barn needing major work
£25–50,000	run-down farm/outbuildings, to restore; or small restored cottage
£50–75,000	restored two- or three-bedroom country house and garden; or similar townhouse
£75–100,000	renovated thee-bedroom country house, plus land; or farm and outbuildings around courtyard, needing work, and 4,000 square metres of land; or large new house on edge of hamlet
£100–150,000	specialist country house with all mod cons and pool; or smart three-storey townhouse
£150–250,000	main residence with converted outbuildings, for possible rental
£250–300,000	superb family home with 2,000 square metres of land, e.g. restored riverside coaching inn
£300,000+	small château, ten bedrooms, and ample land

The familiar façade of a charentaise – overgrown and full of character

Points to consider

The *charentaise* is a good example of the rule of thumb that the more you spend on a property, the more you get for your money pound for pound. For that price, a property is likely to include habitable outbuildings that can generate rental income. Local craftsmen have a good reputation but tend to be booked up well in advance. A commercial enterprise like this is so popular in this area that there are even courses available in how to buy, renovate and run *gîtes*.

budget flights & transport links

FLY TO LIMOGES FROM:
London Stansted (Ryanair)

FLY TO POITIERS FROM:
London Stansted (Ryanair)

FLY TO LA ROCHELLE FROM:
London Stansted (Ryanair)

Charente-Maritime and Charente are served by TGV trains into the area, with stops at Surgères and La Rochelle in

Charente-Maritime and Angoulême and Ruffec in Charente. There is a good network of motorways and main roads within the region, running north–south and east–west, and connecting with airports at La Rochelle, Angoulême, Cognac, Bordeaux, Limoges and Poitiers, and the ferry from the UK to St Malo (less than four hours' drive away to the north in Brittany). A car is essential for rural properties.

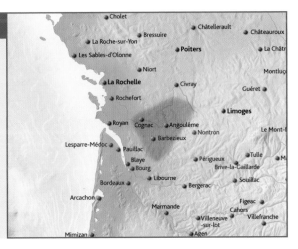

House-hunters

Gilbert Crabtree and Janet Townley
Budget: £115,000

An old winery outside Jarnac with three bedrooms, kitchen, dining room, living room and large spare room. Distillery, barn and 2,000 square metres of garden. **£118,000**

Renovated seventeenth-century townhouse in Confolens with three bedrooms, kitchen, dining room, living room and bathroom. Garden and stone garage. **£101,000**

Caravan holidays in Europe made Gilbert Crabtree and Janet Townley realize that they wanted to put down more permanent roots abroad. Deciding to give up their home on the Isle of Wight, they went to explore the Charente where they hoped to discover a rambling retreat in the sun. Key factors were its proximity to the Channel ports, golf courses and a pool. Their friends and family were already queuing up to visit, so they wanted to be able to accommodate them too.

Property 1

Jarnac is the second most important centre for cognac production. Just outside town was an old limestone winery with plenty of character that had been on the market for the past two years. It was very roomy with a billiards table taking up the living room and a big kitchen table for family eating. The living room had an attractive mezzanine floor that Janet felt could be dangerous without a balustrade; to install one would cost £5,000. The kitchen also had huge floor-to-ceiling kitchen cupboards, one of which hid a door to a surprise secret room and a half-covered, unfinished indoor pool. Gilbert and Janet were staggered. 'We've fallen in love. It's everything I've dreamed of and it's ready to move into.' Gilbert's only reservation was the pool. He preferred the idea of having one in the garden. To dig one out (subject to planning permission), simultaneously using the rubble to fill in the existing one, would cost an estimated £10,000. Because the owners had found a house they wanted to buy, they were anxious for a quick sale, so Gilbert and Janet were recommended to make an opening offer of £95,000 if they were interested.

On balance, though, they felt the extension wasn't in keeping with the rest and they'd prefer to look elsewhere.

Property 2

The next property they saw was in Confolens. Properties in the town's historic centre are hard to come by, those with a river view being high in demand. Inside there was a fully fitted modern kitchen with original exposed beams, and an impressive dining room that led into the living room, complete with working fireplace and wooden floor. The original seventeenth-century staircase led up to the bedrooms that commanded far-reaching views of both river and town. The owner had retained many original features but had updated the décor with bright colours and

modern finishes. The dining room was tiled on the floors and walls as a flood damage limitation exercise. For the same reason, all the sockets were at eye level, with the junction box upstairs, while in the kitchen the cupboards were tiled inside and their doors could be easily removed. The extremes of winter and summer temperatures meant that there were few windows at the front of the building. To have an additional one in the bedroom would need planning permission in this historic conservation area. Janet was enthusiastic. 'The location is to die for. A beautiful kitchen, spacious bedrooms and the garden's so quaint but there's no room for a pool.'

Property 3

They travelled to the foothills of the Massif Central where there was a traditional *charentaise* country home for sale in the tiny village of La Guerlie. Only two minutes from the lakes and ten minutes from the nearest golf course, the property was well under Gilbert and Janet's budget. The long kitchen had exposed beams, a stripped pine floor, a large fireplace and plenty of space for a large table. The living/dining room was doubling as a charming bedroom. A vast unused area under the roof could easily be converted into two bedrooms and a bathroom for an estimated £6,000. The garden was very private and the unused barn was vast. The only drawback was that the owners didn't want to move for seven months, while Gilbert and Janet had given themselves a deadline of four months to get themselves established in a new home.

Two-bedroom charentaise house with kitchen, dining/living room and bathroom. Front and back gardens, vegetable plot and two large barns. **£80,000**

Property 4

Finally they travelled to see a nineteenth-century farmhouse outside Angoulême. Although recently renovated, it did need some finishing touches. The wooden fitted kitchen contained the old stove that had been converted into a cupboard. There was a spacious living area with white walls, exposed beams and tiled floor with a gallery above where windows let in more light. A geothermal underfloor heating system used energy from the natural springs beneath the house. The barn attached to the house was as big as a conventional three-bedroom house. 'This is a delightful property. It's very spacious with well-proportioned rooms. We loved the feel of it.' Although above their budget, there was potential for Gilbert and Janet to convert the outbuildings into *gîtes* to cover the additional outlay. They decided to offer £110,000 but it was not accepted. So Gilbert and Janet had no choice but to hitch up their caravan and continue their search for their perfect home in the sun.

Nineteenth-century farmhouse outside Angoulême with four bedrooms, two bathrooms, kitchen, dining room, living room and cellar. Large garden, barn, two stables and pigeonnière. **£120,000**

Ex-pat experience

Matt and Alison Howard
near Cognac, Charente

The pressures of life in southern England drove golf professional Matt Howard, and his estate agent wife Alison, to France where they set up home two years ago. They found a house in a small hamlet near Cognac where Matt is attached to a local golf club, teaching private clients, and Alison has joined the agency that sold them their home. When they are not busy working professionally, they are both to be found converting their barn into three *gîtes* to generate some additional income.

The estate agent they bought the property from recommended them a surveyor and also builders who tendered for the job. 'There's a lot of scaremongering but it's unfounded. There are more shyster builders in the UK than here, where they come from local villages and have their reputation to protect. They've done excellent work for us and almost on time.'

The Howards believe that life in France today is similar to England during the 1950s. 'Everybody's very trusting. Our neighbour hasn't locked his door for fifteen years. It's a completely different way of life.' Alison's French is fluent, while Matt has taken lessons with a local woman and can now manage perfectly well. They have been welcomed into the local community to the extent that when Matt was painstakingly digging his *potager* (allotment), a local landowner ploughed it for them and lent his rotovator as a favour, saving months of work.

'Learn French as well as you can if you want to be accepted with open arms.'

The food has taken some getting used to. 'The vegetables are always served separately. And the garlic… When we said we liked it, a neighbour put three bulbs into a stew. We thought it would put us off for life.'

Life is relaxed here. So much so that shopping has become a pleasure. With no shops in the village, the Howards have to bicycle to Villefagnan which lies beside an inland lake where they can swim as well. Alternatively, they can go to Ruffec where an English shop offers the delights of Bisto and Marmite, although nowhere can Matt buy a decent pint of real ale. His other comment is the amount of red tape involved in transactions. 'For instance, when you use your car you must have your licence, insurance documents, proof of identity and MOT certificate with you in case you are spot-checked.'

'Have a go at everything on offer. If you involve yourself with the local community, you will be accepted quicker.'

However, that seems a small price to pay for a life where the people are friendly, the cost of living cheaper and the environment exceptional.

Extremadura

Western Spain

On the border of Portugal, Extremadura is remote, almost untouched by tourism or industry, and has some of the cheapest property prices in Spain. The region boasts 300 days of sunshine a year, but while it can be extremely hot in the summer, it is correspondingly bitter in the depths of winter. Its landscape is diverse and beautiful, bordered north and south by mountain ranges with wooded sierras, rolling green fields, forests of pine and cork oak, not forgetting the dozens of picturesque towns and villages that modern development has passed by. The rivers Guadiana and Tajo flow from east to west with magnificent lakes throughout the region. The name Extremadura is believed to mean 'beyond the [River] Duero'.

Once colonized by the Romans, the region still has some fine architectural remains. Alfonso IX won the country back from the Moors in the thirteenth century and divided much of the land among military orders who turned it over to livestock farming. Many of the Spanish conquistadors came from Extremadura and brought back riches from the Americas that briefly transformed the region. Since then prosperity has declined, resulting in rural depopulation as younger generations head away to find work elsewhere.

A typical Extremaduran town is usually less white than those found in Andalucia

websites

www.turismoextremadura.com

Regional Tourist Office
Plaza de la Libertad, 3
Badajoz
Tel: 09 24 22 27 63

Extremadura comes alive with local festivals throughout the year, including Caratoñas (Acehuche, January), when people dress as wild beasts; Los Empaulos (Valverde de la Vera, Holy Week), a procession of penitents; Encamisá (Torrejoncillo, December), when riders parade through town amid bonfires; and Ferias de Cáceres and Trujillo (May, June). Local cuisine derives from two sources: good hearty peasant fare that relies on lamb and home-grown produce; and more sophisticated recipes originating in the monasteries and convents, notably the Convento de Benito in Alcántara. Extremadura is also known for its cured hams, particularly from the village of Montánchez, while the traditional handicrafts of lace-making copperware, jewellery and bee-keeping still continue.

Where to go

The north-east of the region is green and tranquil, with valleys and uplands circling **Plasencia**, an old town that has hosted its busy weekly market since the twelfth century. The Valle de Jerte has some of the most fertile land in the region, growing cherries, raspberries, peanuts and tobacco, but the most important crop is pimiento peppers. Nearby lies the Monfragüe Natural Park, Extremadura's only protected area and home to over 200 animal species including some spectacular birds of prey that can be seen wheeling over the mountain tops.

Mérida is the capital of the region and boasts a superbly preserved Roman theatre among other monuments. Its feel is more reminiscent of towns in neighbouring Andalucía than others further north in the region. The old towns of **Cáceres** and **Trujillo** have changed little since they were built around the sixteenth century. Many of their seigneurial mansions emblazoned with family shields have been passed through generations and are still privately owned. In 1948, Cáceres became Spain's first listed heritage city and is frequently used as a film set. The medieval hill-top town of Trujillo has an irregularly shaped, arcaded Plaza Mayor, its different levels linked by wide flights of steps. At its centre is the statue of its son, the explorer Francisco Pizarro. The surrounding mansions front steep narrow streets lined by frequently whitewashed houses. In the south-west, the other principal city, **Badajoz**, rises up a hill to its ruined Moorish fortress. Its strategic position on the Portuguese border made it the site of many battles but it has long since shaken off the yoke of the past and, while few historic buildings remain, it presents itself as a thriving modern city.

The history of the region is preserved in its towns and villages where architecture and local traditions have stood the test of time. Towns such as **Guadalupe**, **Plasencia** and **Hervás** are among many where centuries slip away in the face of original buildings and a pace of life far removed from the rat race. Medieval churches and cathedrals, monasteries – particularly at Guadalupe and Yuste – and ancient fortified castles all tell their own tales to contribute to the richness and variety that is Extremadura.

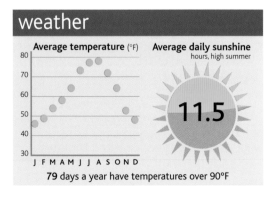

weather

Average temperature (°F)   Average daily sunshine
                            hours, high summer

11.5

80
70
60
50
40
30
J F M A M J J A S O N D

79 days a year have temperatures over 90°F

Property

As yet, few British buyers have discovered the delights of Extremadura, but it is an exciting new area that is opening up thanks to great improvements in road connections with Madrid and a network of new roads that link the old Madrid–Lisbon motorway, as well as the new motorway that is being completed. Not surprisingly, prices go down in the more remote villages and up in those nearer towns and cities.

In the southern area surrounding Frenegal de la Sierra, bordering on the Sierra de Aracena Natural Park the landscape is very green, dotted with lakes and without the high summer temperatures further north. The most suitable properties tend to be village houses simply because the farms are built on a much grander scale than in neighbouring Andalucía, with hundreds of oak trees planted so the black pigs can root out the acorns that give the particular flavour to the ham.

In central Extremadura, the area to the east of Guadalupe is high enough to avoid the heat of the summer that can be fierce on the central plains. Here the huge lakes including Embalse de Cijara and de Garcia de Sola are as yet largely unexploited and there is little population outside the villages. Those such as Herrera del Duque, Orellana la Vieja, Castilblanco and Fuenlabrada de los Montes all have an average of 2,000–3,000 elderly inhabitants. Prices are lower than in the south of the region and there is plenty of opportunity to find houses on the edges of the villages. The whole area has yet to be developed on a rural tourism basis despite its magnificent scenery and the welcoming attitude of its residents.

The castle dominates the ancient village of Albuquerque

Types of property

In the north, village houses again vary in size from small to very big indeed, depending on the wealth of their original owners. Most of them have two or sometimes three floors, many with cellars that were used for storing hams – the local speciality. Many of them have gardens and that of course immediately increases the price. A common feature is the *pasillo*, a wide corridor running from the front gate to the back of the house, either paved in granite or with a central strip of granite. This was to let the animals walk from the street to the stable at the back. The houses are commonly built of granite and roofs are typically wooden with terracotta tiles. Floors can be stone or tiles, sometimes patterned. Other typical features include brick vaults in the rooms on the lower floors, exposed walls on both the exterior and interior of the house, and

interesting facts

❊ The Spanish conquistadors, Pizarro, Cortés, de Soto and de Orellana were among those who came from Extremadura.

❊ Trujillo is also known as 'cradle of conquerors'.

❊ Pimientos that make the finest paprika in Spain were introduced by Christopher Columbus.

❊ The shrine of the virgin at Guadaloupe attracts thousands of pilgrims every year.

❊ The sixth-century temple palace found near Zalamea de la Serena is the only known monument in the world of the Tartessan civilization.

attractive wooden doors that have an opening top quarter for looking out, rather than opening the whole door.

What can you get for your money?

These price bands are a guide to the properties you might find.

£7,000+	building plots
£25–£35,000	two-bedroom cottage in barely habitable condition
£35–50,000	three-/four-bedroom village house in reasonable condition
£50,000+	very good houses on the edge of a village with internal garden/patio and good views of the countryside; or country house with land and swimming pool
£120,000	three-bedroom house with garden overlooking Embalse de Garcia de Sola

Fregenal de la Sierra lies in the foothills of the Sierra Morena

Points to consider

It is possible to buy plots of land (though they may be larger than bargained for) on which to build modern houses. In the north the average cost of house and plot is approximately £400 per square metre, depending on the extent of the works. In villages, it is possible to demolish houses with no intrinsic historic or architectural merit (planning permission required) and rebuild on their footprint. Otherwise it is possible to rebuild while maintaining the original façade. A frequent problem with old houses is that the external walls may be rendered with lime, and the underlying stonework grouted with soil. This leads to extensive damp over time and is expensive to remedy.

budget flights & transport links

FLY TO MADRID FROM:
Birmingham, London Gatwick (British Airways)

London Heathrow (easyJet, Bmibaby)

Liverpool, Luton, Manchester (easyJet)

Dublin (Aer Lingus)

Principal roads are the NV motorway running from Madrid through Trujillo, Mérida to Badajoz; also the N630 from Seville to Mérida, Cáceres and Plasencia. It is easiest to travel by car but there are local bus services and a train link between Madrid, Cáceres and Badajoz.

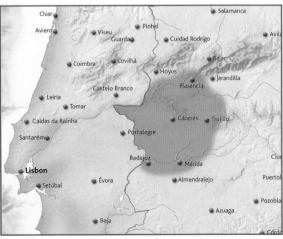

House-hunters

Will and Linda Hammond
Budget: £90,000

Having decided to give up their life in Derbyshire for a new start in Extremadura, social workers Will and Linda Hammond were quite open-minded about the type of property they might buy. 'We'd be happy to renovate provided it wasn't a complete ruin. We want tranquillity and enough land for crops and some animals so we can be self-sufficient.' Will is also a musician so he was hoping to find somewhere where he could work on his projects undisturbed.

Property 1

The first property they visited was an old stone house in the small settlement of Mahincal in the Valle de Jerte. The inside was airy and open with arches leading from the sizeable living room with its attractive exposed stone wall and fireplace to the kitchen that they agreed had potential. They felt the panelled bedroom was on the small side. Outside there was a beautiful pool and plenty of room for ducks, geese and chickens. The property had three wells, one for drinking with water that went through a filter system and two for irrigation. If they chose not to use them, water could be delivered to the property at a cost of £150 per month. Despite it being the right size, and the owner's promise of a gift of chickens and geese, Will and Linda were not convinced that it was right for them.

Two-bedroom stone cottage in the Valle de Jerte with kitchen, living room and bathroom. Large veranda, pool and 4,000 square metres of land. **£55,000**

Property 2

It was on to the outskirts of Montánchez where a rustic *finca* offered extremely basic accommodation but was set in two hectares of land, complete with fig and quince trees and vines. The house itself had a large living area and a washroom that was currently being used as a storeroom. However, because it was set on so much land, planning permission would be forthcoming for an extension that might include five additional rooms plus kitchen and bathroom. An estimate for the work came in at £19,000. There was no telephone line nor electricity but the Hammonds were interested to learn that for £10,000 worth of solar panels, the government, keen to promote their use, would refund £4,000. The owner estimated that three tons of figs were harvested from the land each year. The better news was that a co-operative picked them and

One-bedroom rustic finca *outside Montànchez with living room and washroom. Two hectares of land, including fig plantation.* **£29,000**

he received £2,000 the previous year. Will and Linda liked the prospect of living in such an attractive spot and could see there were lots of positive points about it, but they decided to look further before making up their mind.

Property 3

One of the smartest addresses in the Monfragüe Natural Park is right on the banks of the Playa de Extremadura. Prices here are high thanks to the strict building regulations in the area but the six-bedroom modern villa was a must-see. It was designed and built by the owner and had a cool white interior with one space flowing through into another, built-in sofas, a modern fitted

Six-bedroom modern villa in the Manfragüe Natural Park with three bathrooms, kitchen, living room. Pool, garage and 6,000 sqaure metres. £77,000

kitchen and a master bedroom and ensuite bathroom hidden behind the fitted cupboards. Outside, the pool was invitingly blue. The Hammonds liked what they saw, knowing it was in one of the best locations in Extremadura, close to the river and only a one-and-a-half-hour drive to Madrid. The large garden could be landscaped with an irrigation system installed for around £3,000 but Will and Linda preferred the wildness of it, thinking they had the ability and will to make it into what they wanted. However they were deterred by the fact that there were three nuclear power stations just round the bend from it.

Property 4

Lastly, they visited Arroyo dos Molinos, a quiet village where, in 1811, the British fought with the Spanish against Napoleon's occupying army. The house was unassuming from the outside. But step through the front door and a long cool hall led to a small living room and a bedroom with hams hanging from the ceiling while upstairs the small master bedroom had a balcony overlooking the street. Outside, a lemon tree was growing in the patio surrounded by plenty of flowering pots. Linda was moved to tears by it. 'It's incredible. It's the most

Two-bedroom village house in Arroyo dos Molinos with two reception rooms, study, kitchen and bathroom. Balcony and patio area. £33,000

amazing house I've ever seen. This is it.' Although they had been wanting something more rural, they were delighted to find that it was normal practice for the villagers to have an allotment outside the village where they would grow their own vegetables. Because the owner wanted a quick sale, Will and Linda were advised to put in an opening offer of £29,000 if they were interested.

Although their offer was accepted, the vendors dragged their feet so Will returned and, as luck would have it, found another house in the same street but at the edge of the village with land, animal enclosures and a range of outbuildings. This time things are going smoothly to make a new life in Extremadura.

Ex-pat experience

Philippa Sharman
Montánchez, Extremadura

Twenty years ago, Philippa Sharman took her young daughter, Lucy, to Portugal for a short holiday with her parents and never returned to the UK. 'I began by working as an interior decorator in the Algarve but when I met my husband Manfred, we decided to move to the Alentejo. We turned to *turismo rural* and opened a guest house supported by the Portuguese Tourist Board. Finally we decided to move on having renovated the mill and created a very successful business but we wanted one more big challenge before we became too decrepit.' A new bridge to Lisbon meant property prices were rising and life was changing. Before, their existence had been quiet, rural and very cut off and they hoped to rediscover that quality of life by moving to Extremadura. 'We sold the mill and the goodwill of the business for a fantastic profit. Now we have bought again for a reasonable price and we're sure prices will go up here over the next few years. Extremadura is no longer as remote as it was but retains a marvellous feeling of calm and a peaceful rural life.

'Ask a Spaniard to help you find your way through the bureaucratic processes.'

'We wanted a farmhouse with a big piece of land but those kind of properties are huge here. In the end we bought eight acres with an old barn and we're going to build a *finca* with an activity centre, studio, sitting and dining room. There'll be four large bedrooms for guests, all with private bathrooms, and a swimming pool.' They fell in love with the spectacular location on the slopes of the Sierra Montánchez which, with the ancient Moorish pathways across the mountains, are ideal for trekking. An added bonus is that it is in the middle of the triangle of three World Heritage sites at Cáceres, Mérida and Trujillo.

Their original plans were delayed because they wanted a contemporary building but the local authorities insisted it should imitate traditional local architecture. Now they have a Spanish architect designing a one-storey wood and stone *cortijo* with two floors at one end.

When their house is completed, they will run t'ai chi, art and craft courses, and walking and riding holidays (www.finca-al-manzil.com). At the moment they can make ends meet by living a very simple life where the cost of living is much less than in the UK. They are also encouraged by the Spanish government who will repay 30 per cent of the cost of the project as an incentive, so keen are they to promote rural tourism within the area. With the new motorway from Madrid, the area is opening up for *Madrileños* to buy second homes but few foreigners have yet to take the plunge.

'Nobody speaks English here, so it's essential to take Spanish lessons.'

Philippa and Manfred have experienced little difficulty in getting their project off the ground: 'There is a lot of bureaucratic stuff but it is not impossible to deal with. Getting builders was easy. They're busy but not extraordinarily so. So you can book them for when you've received your licenses.' The local people have been friendly too. 'We feel very happy here. People chat in the street to us. It's so charming, even if we only understand half of what they say.'

Champagne

Champagne-Ardennes, France

Away from the vineyards, the towns and villages of Champagne, such as Domange, are surrounded by vast agricultural plains

The lure of the bubbly stuff has attracted people to the region of Champagne since the eighteenth century, when a blind monk, Dom Pérignon, is reputed to have created it by accident. But there is far more than that to be enjoyed here.

Champagne-Ardenne is in the north-east of France, only a short drive from Paris, and is made up of four departments: Ardennes, Marne, Aube and Haute-Marne, the last three of which comprise the Champagne region. In the north-west stretch acres of vineyards, while elsewhere the rivers Seine, Aube, Aisne, Meuse and Marne cut through vast windswept fields or thickly forested country-side. The prevalent limestone chalk contributes towards the right conditions for producing champagne. Near Troyes the great lakes of Aube – the Lac d'Orient, Lac du Temple and Lac Amance – and Marne's Lac du Der-Chantecoq provide endless opportunities for sailing, swimming, fishing and birdwatching, while the flat terrain makes for comfortable cycling.

Food comes a close second to drink in Champagne, some specialities being the *andouillette* sausages from Troyes, meat dishes marinaded in champagne, *potée champenoise* (hotpot of ham sausage and bacon with lashings of cabbage) and cheese such as *chaource, cendré, mostafait* and *troyat*. Traditional crafts include glass-making, especially crystal, ceramic and enamel production, leatherware and papermaking, while among the most noteworthy festivals are the Troyes' ham festival (Easter), Troyes' champagne festival (June), the Fêtes Johanniques and Les Sacres du Folklore (Reims, June).

highlights

❊ The Champagne Route

❊ The old town of Troyes

❊ Reims' cathedral

❊ Champagne's timber churches near Lac du Der-Chantecoq

❊ The Forêt d'Orient and the Montagne de Reims Regional Nature Parks

Where to go

The principal city, **Reims**, is twinned with Canterbury and famed for its superb Notre-Dame Cathedral used for French coronations between the eleventh and eighteenth centuries. The cathedral is one of four UNESCO world heritage sites in the city, the others being the Tau Palace, the Saint Remi Basilica and the Saint Remi Museum. Surrounded by vineyards and wheatfields, Reims is at the centre of champagne production, with the well-preserved fortified town of **Epernay**. Beneath both towns spread vast cellars cool enough for manufacturing millions of gallons of champagne. **Châlons-en-Champagne** (previously Châlons-sur-Marne) was once the main town of the region and remains its administrative centre. Less well known than Reims and Epernay as a champagne-producing town, it nonetheless boasts a number of prestigious labels. Built across the Mau and Nau canals, the historic centre has well-preserved mansions and medieval half-timbered houses, as well as a gothic cathedral and a number of churches.

Troyes is thought by many to be Champagne's most beautiful city. It dates back to Roman times and was a prosperous trading centre in the Middle Ages. The British captured the city in the fifteenth century but it was soon liberated by Joan of Arc. Its cobbled streets are lined with half-timbered medieval and Renaissance buildings, and its gothic cathedral has one of the largest stained-glass windows in France. To the west of the town lies the peaceful countryside of the Pays d'Othe, an important cider-producing area with over 35,000 acres of woodland dotted with twenty quiet villages.

To the south of the region, perched high on a rocky spur, is **Chaumont**, once the home of the Counts of Champagne and noted for its magnificent nineteenth-century railway viaduct. In the narrow streets of the old town, Renaissance houses still have their turreted staircases and carved doors. Close by is the massive Cross of Lorraine, symbol of the French Resistance movement, on a hill west of Colombey-les-Deux-Eglises, once the home of General de Gaulle. South again is the ancient bishopric of **Langres**, superbly sited on a plateau's edge and claiming its proximity to the sources of the Seine and Marne as a source of mystical powers. Apart from its cathedral, the highlight of the town is the panoramic view from its ramparts.

The weather may not be Mediterranean, but there are attractive villages, historic buildings, castles, monasteries, churches and museums, superb cycling and walking country, plenty of opportunities for outdoor activities *and* the drink of kings – all within easy reach of the UK.

websites

www.notaires.fr
gives typical house prices throughout France

www. champagne.fr
the official website of the champagne wines

www.tourisme-champagne-ardenne.com
the official website of the Champagne-Ardenne tourist board

weather

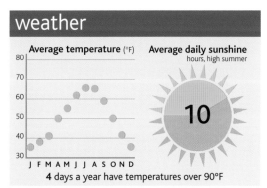

Average temperature (°F) **Average daily sunshine** hours, high summer

10

J F M A M J J A S O N D

4 days a year have temperatures over 90°F

Property

Cuis is another typical historical village surrounded by vineyards

Property prices in Champagne are on the rise. Over the last five years they have gone up by 30 per cent, in the last two by 20 per cent. Although British home-buyers are just discovering the area, it has long been a favourite area for Parisians, both for weekend hideaways and for principal residences since it is only an hour and a half's train ride from the capital. Because of the state of the economy, the French are investing their money in property; with its variety and accessibility, Champagne is attracting more and more visitors each year.

Types of property

There are four main types of architecture in the region. In or close to the towns are two- or three-storey mansions built with large limestone blocks, surrounded by substantial walled grounds. Inside there may be huge fireplaces dating back to Renaissance times, and elegant wooden floors. The rooms are spacious with high ceilings and tall windows.

Farmhouses are often built round a courtyard. They are usually modest buildings made of smaller stones and with a number of attached outbuildings or stables that make them ideal for renovating into *gîtes* or *chambres d'hôte*. The interiors of the main houses are naturally more modest than the mansions, typically with simple wooden floors, stone fireplaces and smaller rooms. Frequently there is a loft that would once have been used for storing grain. These have great potential as additional bedrooms and bathrooms. Village houses are simpler still, frequently being only one storey with a front or back yard.

Finally, there are the houses built using *columbage* or *pan de bois*. These are half-timbered houses that were constructed with a wooden frame and wattle infill. Although this technique is no longer used in building, it is still possible to find historic properties on the market. In the country these are generally single-storey buildings but in the towns they have several floors, with the upper ones jutting out over the street. The very best examples of the latter are to be found in the city of Troyes. Because of the way they are constructed, the windows are generally on the small side and that means dark interiors.

Another popular buy are the windmills that are to be found in the flatter parts of the region. They can be converted into unusual homes with plenty of character. In any of these properties, typical features might include original fireplaces, exposed wooden ceiling beams, and stone or wooden floors. All of these can vary from simple to elaborate, depending on the wealth of the original owner and the period the property was built.

interesting facts

❋ Before champagne, Champagne was famous for its red wines.

❋ The region produces over 300 million bottles of champagne a year.

❋ There are 6, 300 square metres of stained glass in the department of Aube alone.

❋ Only champagne produced in this region of France can be called 'champagne'.

❋ 33 per cent of France's socks are produced in Troyes.

What can you get for your money?

These price bands are a guide to the properties you might find.

£30,000+	farms for renovation, though these are becoming increasingly hard to find
£70,000+	renovated stone or brick village houses; new four-bedroom houses with nearly 1,000 square metres of land in the Aube district
£100–130,000	renovated farmhouse
£130–170,000	eighteenth-century *maison bourgeoise* (large family house), with 4–5,000 square metres of land
£100–170,000	new-build villa; at the top end with four bedrooms, the house covering about 200 square metres
£130,000+	converted farmhouses/country houses with pool and land

The village of Cumières is close to Epernay in the heart of champagne country

Points to consider

Prices vary according to the region. Popular areas with incomers are the Forêt d'Othe, le Chaource, Bar-sur-Seine and Haute-Marne. The north of Aube is cheaper than the south simply because the countryside is deemed prettier the further south you go. The most northerly department, Marne, is more expensive than both Aube or Haute-Marne, and the closer to Reims, the pricier it becomes. As a comparison, a three-bedroom in the Troyes area might fetch £34,000 whereas its equivalent in Marne would be around £50,000. Gorgeous country houses can be found for the price of a town apartment, so it pays to do your homework before you look.

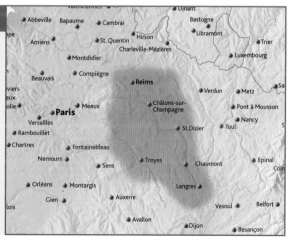

budget flights & transport links

FLY TO REIMS FROM:
London Stansted (Ryanair)

The main roads running through the region are the A4 from Alsace west through Reims to Paris, the A26 from St Quentin south through Reims to Troyes, and the A5 from Troyes south through Langres towards Dijon. The rail services are good, as are most of the minor roads.

House-hunters

Dave and Wendy Southwell
Budget: £90,000

Running a B&B in Skegness had given Dave and Wendy Southwell the confidence to run a similar business in France. That, combined with their many holidays caravanning through the country, had led them to Champagne. 'We love this area and the way of life here. We're looking for a large family house but we need to earn a living too, so we are thinking of running a B&B or a campsite.'

Six-bedroom eighteenth-century house outside Troyes, with two bathrooms, kitchen and living room. 2,000 square metres of land. **£79,000**

Five-bedroom renovated house in the Forêt d'Othe with kitchen, bathroom, living room. Heated swimming pool, covered BBQ area, 2,000 square metres of land with vegetable garden. **£118,000**

Property 1

They started their search with an eighteenth-century house just outside Troyes that had the potential to be converted into a *chambre d'hôte*. The impressive gateway led into a characteristic courtyard and round to a typically French garden complete with apple and cherry trees and a strawberry patch. Inside, the airy living room had a corner fireplace and large windows with a view of the garden. The traditional French kitchen was a good size, with original terracotta floor tiles and a dedicated cheese safe. The master bedroom had a small children's bedroom off it. Considering how they could use the house, the Southwells saw the possibility of converting the two front rooms into self-contained flats. Both the kitchen and bathroom were pretty basic and had damp so they would also have to be renovated to bring them up to standard. All that work would cost £20–30,000.

Although the building was not listed, any interior or exterior structural changes would have to be approved by the mayor. However, the mayor was known to be keen to see the building converted into a *chambre d'hôte*, so this was unlikely to be problem. Overall, Dave and Wendy thought that, however lovely, it was not quite big enough for them and needed too much work.

Property 2

Next, they headed south to the Forêt d'Othe where a recently renovated house, once belonging to a countess, was on the market. There was an enormous family living room with original fireplace, a fully fitted wooden kitchen with blue-tile worktops and splashbacks. The large master bedroom had another fabulous fireplace and big windows, while the children's room in the attic had dormer windows and heavy ceiling beams. 'The house is wonderful – exactly what we imagined we might find. A perfect mix of original and modern features.' Dave was keen

on converting the garden into a caravan site until he was told of the strict rules governing such matters: 90 square metres of land has to be allowed per caravan or tent, which meant that they could comfortably accommodate only four.

Having to build the necessary amenities of shower and toilet blocks for so few meant it might not be a financially viable project. However, if they converted the loft into three bedrooms and a bathroom they would have a total of five lettable rooms. Given the house's history and its stunning heated pool, they should be able to expect £50 per night for bed and breakfast.

Property 3

Then they visited a farmhouse close to the ancient spa town of Aix-en-Othe. Renovated twenty years earlier, the property was within their budget and had plenty of potential for creating the extra accommodation they wanted. The cosy living room had a stone fireplace and original beams. The L-shaped kitchen led into the dining room that had a beamed ceiling and floor-to-ceiling windows with views to the garden. One of the bathrooms was on the same floor. Upstairs there were two attic bedrooms, perfect for conversion, and a vast master bedroom that could sleep six. Converting the loft into three bedrooms with kitchen and bathroom would cost £10,000. Dave was particularly taken with the idea that he might buy a neighbouring orchard that would take twenty caravans. It already had planning permission so he would be able to build the amenity blocks. Nonetheless, they did not feel the house was quite right for them.

Three-bedroom farmhouse near Aix-en-Othe with kitchen, bathroom, two reception rooms and spacious loft area. 4,000 square metres of mature garden. **£88,000**

Converted flour mill on the Champagne Route with three double bedrooms, two kitchens, pantry, living room, study and cellar. Outbuildings including garage, barn and stable. Two hectares. **£99,000**

Property 4

Lastly, they saw a mill near Sézanne. The rooms were all enormous, with many original features. Looking beyond the floral wallpaper, they could see the potential for creating six *gîtes* for £100,000. But the really attractive thing was the outside space where Dave could envisage his perfect campsite. It would take £12,000 to build the amenity blocks to service up to fifty caravans. It was a huge project, but one they could imagine carrying out gradually over the years.

Both Wendy and Dave were excited about the second and fourth properties they had seen. They went for a second viewing of both, even taking Wendy's parents with them. Although finally deciding that neither was quite right after all, they did decide that they wanted to go on looking for the ideal property in Champagne or nearby.

Ex-pat experience

Susan Guillerand
Arsonval, Aube, Champagne

Bernard and Susan Guillerand with their daughter, Emma

Susan Guillerand was working in the hotel and catering business when she met her husband Bernard, a chef in the Stratford Hilton. For a time they lived and worked in Paris but then in 1977 decided they wanted to open their own business. Bernard's parents lived in Champagne and spotted a ruined country house in a lovely setting, and lent them the money to buy it. 'It had been turned into a hotel between the wars but had been badly neglected over the years. The kitchen was alive with rats, and there were no main drains.' After trying to battle with it themselves, they took out a mortgage to finance the major repairs including a new roof. Later they renovated the dilapidated coach house into bedrooms and added a panoramic dining room at the back of the hotel. 'We couldn't knock it down because it was a classified building so, after a lot of bureaucracy and paperwork, we got a grant for the renovation.' Twenty-six years since they began, L'Hostellerie de la Chaumière is still enjoying its revival.

Susan has seen the region change in a number of ways over the years. 'When we first came, Champagne wasn't in very good financial shape. But over the last twenty-five years the wine business has picked up, which has meant more money has come in and there have been some very extravagant houses built by the wine merchants. The roads have always been good but various motorways have been built as well as the artificial lakes.' As a result tourism has increased and consequently so has their business.

> 'Living here means getting back to England is quick and easy – only a two-hour drive from Paris and a three-and-a half-hour drive to Calais.'

> 'For wine experts, we are in the south of the Champagne area between the two Burgundy areas – an hour from Chablis and a good hour from Dijon leading on to the wine route to Beaune.'

When Susan came to France, she quickly adapted to her new life. 'I'm very easy-going and the French accepted me at once. Once we arrived, my husband's family all came over to take a look but it was fine. I've never been made to feel out of things although, of course, you can never really become part of a small village even when you are French.' They were helped by her parents who came to muck in twice a year. 'My father became quite a personality in the village, causing havoc in the DIY shop with his ruler in inches.' Susan has lived in France for so long that there's nothing about England she misses.

What she dislikes most about her life in Champagne is the way their working life prevents them from making many close friends. 'Of course we have acquaintances but all my really good friends are still the people I was at school with.' However, England is within easy reach, as is her daughter Emma in Paris. 'The weather is better here than in England and there is so much space. We do live in such a beautiful setting that visiting Brits all think it's paradise.'

How to buy a property in France

A general guide

It is recommended that you take professional advice to check the contracts you are signing. It is also important to decide in whose name the deed should be registered because of the inheritance implications, and whether or not to make a French will.

The sale of property is strictly regulated in France and conducted by the *notaire* who represents neither the buyer nor the seller. If in any doubt about the procedures, it would be wise to find a solicitor who can explain them to you. Either ask your *agent immobilier* for a recommendation or engage one from a specialist firm in Britain. If you are buying a flat or a new property then there will be variations in the procedure that your lawyer should be able to explain to you.

Exchanging contracts

The estate agent (or occasionally a *notaire*) will draw up a *compromis de vente*, which is a binding legal document recording the agreement to buy and sell between the vendor and the buyer. This document will include both parties' names – though it may be advisable to include a substitution clause to allow another person or company to be inserted after questions of inheritance or taxation have been investigated thoroughly. The precise details of what is being sold should be spelled out. The purchase price, deposit and any additional fees will be mentioned. It will state that the vendor is not responsible for any defects in the property – so make sure you've done your homework. There will also be *conditions suspensives* (conditional clauses) to be satisfied before the deal goes through. These will exempt you from going through with the purchase if, for example, you fail to obtain a mortgage, if the existing mortgage cannot be repaid from the sale, if you cannot obtain clear title to the property, if the boundaries are unclear, or if there are building restrictions on the land. If any of these are not satisfied then your deposit will be returned and the sale cancelled. If, on the other hand, a purchase fails through the buyer's fault, then he will forfeit the deposit.

The contract also specifies a date for completion. After signing the *compromis*, there is a seven-day cooling-off period during which the buyer can back out of the deal without any comeback. Once this period is over, the buyer is committed to the purchase provided all conditions are fulfilled. In some cases, a *promesse de vente* may be used instead. This is an agreement in which the vendor sets out the details of the sale. Once the buyer agrees, the effect is the same as a *compromis*. A deposit of 10 per cent is paid to the *notaire* (or, very occasionally, to the estate agent) who puts it into escrow (an independent third-party account) until completion. The *notaire* must conduct various searches and enquiries with the local authority and land charges registry but these relate to the property alone, not to its surroundings. It is up to you/your solicitor to conduct investigations into general planning proposals for the area to discover if a motorway is planned to run nearby or if a block of flats is to be built in the neighbouring field.

Completing the contract

When the *notaire* has completed his work he will draw up an *acte de vente* which, when signed, completes the transfer of property to the buyer. At this point the balance of the money is due, so the bank transfers need to have been arranged ahead. The buyer is then issued with an *attestation*, a certificate proving they are the owner of the property. The title deeds stay with the *notaire*, but a copy should be sent to the buyer within about three months. Land registry is proof of ownership.

Additional fees

Remember the buyer is responsible for paying both the legal costs and taxes relating to the purchase. If the property has been built within the last five years, the notary's fees will be between 2 and 3 per cent of the purchase price, whereas if it is older, expect his fees to be between 7 and 9 per cent. This covers you for stamp duty, land registry and conveyancing. There is nothing more to pay.

Mountains

'It is a fine thing to be out on the hills alone. A man can hardly be a beast or a fool alone on a great mountain.'

Francis Kilvert 1840-79

Las Alpujarras

Andalucía, Spain

The unspoiled village of Bubión sits among the terraces of the Poquiera valley

A very different world exists just a ninety-minute drive inland from Málaga and the heavily developed Costa del Sol, or a mere thirty minutes east of Granada. Sandwiched between the snow-capped ranges of the Sierra Nevada and the lower Sierras de Lújar, Contraviesa and Gádor lie the Alpujarras, a region of spectacular natural beauty that is steeped in history and tradition. The name Alpujarras comes from *alp* meaning 'high place' and *Ujar* meaning 'goddess of light'. Up here the air is clear and the climate generally warm and sunny; in winter the weather can be unpredictable, with snow falling on the higher slopes. The Gaudalfeo river runs the length of the broad valley, with smaller rivers running down from the Sierra Nevada cutting gorges into the soft terrain and ensuring the region below is fertile. Its isolated location has meant that its traditional character has survived largely undisturbed over the years. Groves of citrus, olive and almond trees blanket hillsides peppered by over seventy picturesque white villages that date back hundreds of years to Moorish times.

In 1492, Boabdil, the last Moorish ruler of Granada, surrendered the city to the Spanish monarchs Ferdinand and Isabella. In return he was given the Alpujarras as a personal fiefdom. Its most western point is marked by the Puerto del Suspiro del Moro (the Pass of the Moor's Sigh), where Boabdil turned back for a final glimpse of Granada. Before they were finally expelled by the Christians, the Moors made an enduring mark on the Alpujarran landscape, with their terracing, irrigation systems and hill-top villages. Gradually rural poverty overran the area until the middle of the twentieth century, when life was breathed back into the Alpujarras, largely by tourism and a number of northern Europeans who came to live here.

Where to go

Lanjarón is a popular resort in the western Alpujarras, renowned for its spa waters that are bottled and sold throughout Spain. The baths are open between March and December, when the shops peddle plenty of herbal remedies to visitors seeking cures. On its outskirts are the remains of a Moorish castle, scene of the Moors' last stand against the Spanish troops. East of Lanjarón is **Orgiva**, the administrative centre of the region and home to a regular Thursday outdoor market that attracts locals as well as the New Age travellers who have made their home in El Beneficio, a nearby commune.

Perhaps the most picturesque villages of all, now firmly part of the tourist trail, are the three suspended above the Poqueira Gorge: **Pampaneira**, **Bubión** and **Capileira**. Further north-east is **Trevélez**, alleged by some to be the highest village in Spain and the best starting point for the ascent of its highest mountain, Mulhacén. The local speciality is its *jamón serrano* (cured mountain ham), famed throughout Spain. Further south the villages of **La Tahá** have a different atmosphere. Off the tourist beat, their sleepy streets offer the authentic characteristics of the Moorish architecture.

East of Trevélez, the attractive village of **Cádiar**, with its stone church, bi-monthly market and lively October cattle and wine fair, lies on the fringe of a more arid landscape. As it levels out, the villages become less frequent, the most eastern of them being **Laujar de Andarax**. Surrounded by vine-yards, there is local wine to sample alongside the cheeses. Throughout the many villages, weaving work-shops produce characteristic cotton rugs. Otherwise there is first-class olive oil, goats' cheese, honey, and baskets woven from esparto grass.

The Alpujarras are part of traditional Spain where the pace of life is relaxed, the surroundings largely unspoilt by the demands of tourism and the cost of living is low. It also offers plenty of opportunities for outdoor pursuits. Within easy reach of Granada and Málaga's airports, Las Alpujarras offers an alternative way of life.

highlights

* The Poqueira Valley
* The Alhambra and other Moorish legacies in Granada
* The majestic peaks of the Sierra Nevada
* The natural carbonated mineral waters at Fuente Agria
* Lanjarón's annual festival and water battle

websites

www.andalucia.com for a general guide to the area and beyond

www.lasalpujarras.com for a guide to local amenities

www.global-spirit.com/alpujarras for bus and train timetables, maps of the area, flight and weather information, activities available

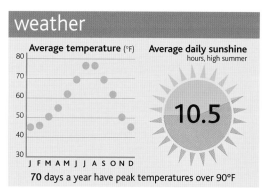

weather

Average temperature (°F)

Average daily sunshine hours, high summer

10.5

J F M A M J J A S O N D

70 days a year have peak temperatures over 90°F

A simple Andalucian farmhouse surrounded by citrus trees and unspoilt countryside

Property

The region is still relatively unspoilt and reasonably cheap by UK standards, but it is no longer a backwater, and property prices are rising fast. In some cases they have doubled, or even trebled, largely through the knock-on effect of rocketing value of coastal properties driving potential home-buyers inland.

Types of property

A major part of the Moorish legacy in the countryside is the architecture: large, square, stone-walled houses with small windows and internal shutters, sometimes built around a courtyard or farmyard. The flat slate roofs, with chestnut or poplar beams, are topped with waterproof clay.

Village houses tend to be more recent, from the seventeenth century to the present day. An attractive feature of village architecture is the *tinao*, a sort of bridge built at first-floor level between two parts of a house on opposite sides of the street. There is usually at least one room on the bridge above the street. The common factor between country and townhouses is that they all have thick walls (up to one metre deep), to keep them cool in summer and warm in winter.

There are few small *cortijos*, or country farmhouses. Most are fairly large, about 100–200 square metres, with six to eight rooms and five hectares or more of land.

What can you get for your money?

These price bands are a guide to the properties you might find.

£20–£35,000	small building site, land only
£35–£50,000	farmhouse needing complete renovation, and five hectares of land
£50–£70,000	village house, unmodernized, plus small garden
£70–£75,000	farmhouse, basic, with land, ready to occupy
£75–£110,000	farmhouse, completely modernized, with land
£110–£170,000	village/townhouse, completely renovated

Points to consider

As a rule of thumb, allow £200–£400 per square metre of house for complete renovation, including bathroom and kitchen, roof and flooring. If considering a new house, make sure that the walls are very thick, for the weather can be cold in winter and unbearably hot in summer. Access for oil trucks can be difficult, so heating tends to be by wood-burning stove or open fire.

interesting facts

❖ Many spaghetti westerns were filmed in the desert-like eastern Alpujarras.

❖ The town of Lanjarón, famous for its spa waters, gives its name to one of Spain's best-known bottled waters.

❖ British writer Gerald Brenan settled in Yégen.

❖ Sel Ling (Place of Clear Light) is a Buddhist retreat perched above the Poquiera Gorge.

Water is a precious commodity and swimming pools are unusual (and often frowned upon). Check water rights and seasonal availability, from mains or springs, carefully before buying. Hours for using the hillside irrigation systems are reduced during dry spells. Mains electricity can also be a problem. In some places it does not exist – likewise, phone connections.

Larger villages have well-stocked shops, and some bakeries deliver bread to your door and groceries by arrangement. Supermarkets are dotted around the area and hypermarkets on the coast carry most UK goods.

The region rates highly for health and education. There are twenty-four-hour accident and emergency centres in Cádiar, Orgiva and Ugijar. An air ambulance service is available for emergencies, carrying patients to hospitals in Granada and Motril. Primary, secondary and technical schools are now used to pupils whose first language is English. They are obliged to run Spanish-language classes if there are sufficient numbers. The nearest international school is in Almuñecar on the coast.

British ex-pats have settled comfortably into the region, despite the understandable niggle about pricing locals out of the housing market. It can cause resentment when incomers pay top whack for a pig farm to convert into residential property, which would otherwise provide employment for eight local people.

Both Cádiar and Yégen boast British-run bars, which tend to be the focal point for the region's English-speaking community. Local newsagents now sell UK newspapers – a sign of the times.

The famed pueblos blancos *of the Alpujarras typically sport wrought iron grilles and blinds to keep out the blazing sun*

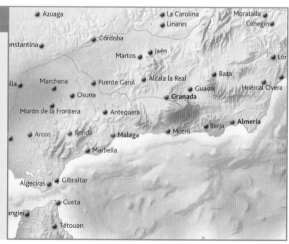

budget flights & transport links

FLY TO MALAGA FROM:
Manchester, Cardiff and East Midlands (Bmibaby)
London Luton, London Gatwick, London Stansted, East Midlands, Liverpool, Bristol City (easyJet)
London Gatwick, Manchester, London Luton, Birmingham, Edinburgh (Monarch)
Southampton (Flybe)

FLY TO ALMERIA FROM:
Dublin (Ryanair)
London Gatwick (Monarch)

There are two main routes from Málaga airport (the nearest village is about 93 miles away): either along the coast via N340 (busy in summer and at Easter) and then turning north after 47 miles; or via Granada and then dropping south via N331 and N332.

Buses connect villages with towns, and towns with cities. Most larger villages have at least an early bus to and from Granada to the north or Almería on the coast, and possibly another later in the day.

House-hunters

Barry Charles and Liz Citron
Budget: £50,000

A two-bedroom house in Mairena, with two reception rooms, kitchen, bathroom, three ground-floor workshops. Terrace. Needs renovation.
£21,000

The Alpujarras are a world away from South London. That is exactly why builder Barry Charles and his partner, marketing director Liz Citron, decided to search there for their second home. Their only provisos were that he wanted a garden where he could try his hand at growing vegetables for the first time and they both wanted a property where they could do some work.

Property 1

The first they saw was in the Yator Valley, just 40 miles from the desert. At 1,800 metres, Mairena is one of the highest villages in Europe. It is of typical Moorish design and immaculately cared for by its mostly elderly residents. In the past three years, six foreign couples have moved here. The thick walls of the two-bedroom village house meant it would be cool inside during the summer. The interior was spacious, with original features including a pair of internal glass doors. The challenge was the three workshops that were completely untouched. The space had great potential but no windows. Local planning law said that they could be put in only if the land they would overlook belonged to the house. The two plots by the house were for sale. The one further away was on the market for £3,500; the nearer one was owned by four brothers, three of whom wanted to sell, one of whom did not. If Barry and Liz offered £4,000, he might be persuaded. The property had bags of personality and potential with the added bonus of daily visits to the village by a baker, fishmonger, bottled-gas seller and beer seller.

Property 2

It was on to the Sierra Nevada Nature Park, a protected area high in the mountains that is extremely beautiful and remote. The one-bedroom *finca* offered a cool traditional living room with stone floors and a traditional brick fireplace. The best bit, apart from the terrace, the land and the panoramic views, was the planning permission to extend the property by two-thirds its size. Liz was attracted by its isolation, while Barry was contemplating the challenge of the large landscaped garden that had grown wild. In the end they felt that it was perhaps a little too isolated for them.

A one-bedroom finca *in the Sierra Nevada Natural Park, with open-plan living room/kitchen, bathroom. Three hectares of land.* **£49,000**

Property 3

Next was a three-bedroom house in the narrow streets of Yégen. Over 130 years old, it had been recently renovated by local craftsmen using local materials. The open-plan living room had a wood-burning fire and views across the rooftops. The floors were all handmade terracotta tiles from a neighbouring village. The kitchen was fully fitted with a gas hob and electric oven with marble worktop. The master bedroom featured original chestnut beams, while a top-floor bedroom led out on to its own courtyard. Barry admired the quality of workmanship but was

An immaculate three-bedroom townhouse in Yégen, with three bathrooms, kitchen, living room and balcony and store room. Large terrace and walled garden. £60,000

disappointed there was no garden. However, he could buy a one-hectare plot outside the village for £4,000. The asking price had been dropped by £3,000 since going on the market six months earlier. However, they decided the property was too perfect to be much of a project for them.

Property 4

Lastly, they visited Orgiva, whose ageing population and traditional way of life were transformed by the arrival of New Age travellers and hippies. Now the town is a lively cosmopolitan centre with shops full of arts, crafts and alternative medicines. The influx of foreigners has pushed up property prices, making Orgiva one of the most expensive places in the Alpujarras. On the edge of town was a large, rambling two-bedroom villa with a new wooden floor in the spacious living room, a snug red-painted study, and a large kitchen with terracotta floor. The beamed master bedroom had French doors leading to a

balcony. Outside, there was a large terrace, a landscaped garden and a pool that needed only cleaning and filling. An irrigation system brought spring water to the garden for twelve minutes each week – enough to water the plants and fill the pool. Barry and Liz liked it immediately. 'It's the sort of house you expect to see when you come to Spain. It has all the right elements, a bit run down but not wildly so, so it suits us both.'

A two-bedroom country house outside Orgiva, with a large open-plan kitchen/diner, living room, bathroom, study. Balconies, terrace, large garden and pool. £91,000

Their dilemma was choosing between the first and fourth properties. In the end they decided to continue looking rather than commit to either of these. As luck would have it, they found a house in a tiny village called Otivar, which is in the same region but closer to the sea. They snapped it up for just £26,000 and are now looking forward to enjoying their new holiday home.

Ex-pat experience

Clare Sasada

El Nido, Orgiva

Seventeen years ago, Clare Sasada drove food and furniture down to the Alpujarras for a friend moving there. Before she knew where she was, she had begun a small removals business. 'It wasn't long before I started a wholefood shop in Orgiva to supply flour, porridge oats and healthy food that was difficult to get here. I set it up from home and was open two days a week. We didn't have phones but there were fewer people and they just passed the word around.'

Clare ran the shop until four years ago, by which time it was a flourishing business. Having sold it, she and her partner Ainsley Platt set up an internet and web hosting business. When that didn't take off, they took a year out to concentrate on their holiday home, El Nido (www.elnido.co.uk), and Clare retrained as a reflexologist in Spain. Now they have opened El Bambú, a restaurant specializing in Thai and vegetarian meals which are all freshly prepared. 'I've lived here so long, the locals know me and have accepted me into the local way of life, but some do not understand what we're doing. Every night one old boy knocks on the door at 6 p.m. for his regular glass of wine and is puzzled why the bar's not open. Some of the locals still have a small-town mentality.'

'Before moving, come and live here for a year to see how the place works and if you like it.'

Clare was one of the first to get a telephone in the area, though most of her neighbours are still reliant on mobiles because the telegraph company will not put up any more posts. There has been a huge influx of northern Europeans to the area. 'People who come now are often retirees and families looking for a better education and way of life for their children. They are restoring derelict properties to live in and the Spanish love seeing the land being looked after again and the return of family life.'

As farming has become more difficult, many locals have turned to the construction business both here and on the coast for work. The motorway is getting closer and the environment is changing too. 'Over the last ten years it has become more seasonal, with winters becoming longer and colder which is at least good for the land.'

Another thing to get used to is the Spanish system of doing things. 'The bureaucracy is frustrating, particularly because the law always seems to be changing.' Another minus is the difficulty of getting people to do things for you. 'With so much construction work going on, the builders, plumbers and electricians are always busy. When you manage to find someone to help, you can explain exactly what you want, they nod and do exactly what they think should be done.'

'Speak some Spanish. If you forget your inhibitions and have a go, everyone will help and you'll learn quickly.'

But the advantages of living here more than outweigh the disadvantages. 'We bought our house four years ago and although there's still work to do, it's comfortable and surrounded by gardens, fields and olive trees. One of the best things is getting up in the morning with the sun shining, picking oranges from the tree to squeeze for breakfast and taking the dogs for a walk. There are no time pressures here, it's not as wet and cold as the UK and the quality of life is much more pleasant.'

The French Pyrenees

T he Pyrenees form a natural boundary between France and Spain, and are the second-largest mountain range in Europe. Just like the Alps, they have peaks of up to 10,000 feet and dozens of ski resorts catering for all levels. The western part of the Pyrenees is known as the Pyrénées-Atlantiques, and is one of the most diversified departments in France, with enormous variations in landscape and weather, architecture and property prices. The big difference between this region and the Alps is that it also has 30 miles of sandy coastline packed with lively resorts. The Pyrénées-Atlantiques also includes part of the Basque region. The Basques are one of Europe's oldest races and are known to have been in the area since the sixth century. Although they lost a good deal of autonomy over the centuries, their strong sense of nationalism re-emerged at the time of the Spanish Civil War (1936–9), leading to the preservation of their language and traditions to this day. The historic game of pelota is still widely played, while bullfights and even bull running are regular entertainments. The Musée Basque in Bayonne is a good starting point to find out more.

Where to go

To the north on the coast lies **Biarritz**, the surfing capital of Europe and a major draw for the international jet set who began coming here in the mid-nineteenth century when Napoleon III and his wife Eugénie visited. Now the town is extremely expensive, but worth visiting for its excellent beaches, which include

Many of the wooden shutters in the old town of Bayonne are painted the characteristic Basque colours of green and red

websites

www.touradour.com
for good maps, history, tourism, hotels

www.pyrenees-atlantiques.com a superb website packed with local information (in French)

www.tourisme.fr
for links to all l ocal tourism and information offices

A lone farmhouse in the fertile countryside of the Pays Basque

the surfing beach at Anglet, for the view from the Rocher de la Vierge, a rocky promontory that juts into the sea, and for the chance to hang out in the many attractive restaurants and bars.

However, the capital of the region is **Bayonne**, known for its smoked ham (a celebratory ham fair is held at Easter), spicy sausage, marzipan and chocolate. Unlike its neighbour Biarritz, it has retained its Basque character through both its architecture and the use of the Basque language. Its medieval Cathédrale Sainte-Marie is the focus of a busy pedestrian area with plenty of cafés selling hot chocolate, the local speciality. Further south along the coast lies the quiet fishing village of **St-Jean-de-Luz**, which is transformed into a tourist hot spot during the summer. A little inland, the walled town of **St-Jean-Pied-de-Port** marked the last stop in France for pilgrims making their way to Santiago de Compostela.

Venturing inland, the landscape changes. The high peaks of the Pyrenees dominate the skyline, but lower down are thick forests and green meadows peppered with tiny hamlets offering remote bolt holes for those who want to get away from it all. The Haut Béarn is part of the Parc National des Pyrénées (Pyrenees National Park). The cattle here are unfenced and are tracked down by the melodic sound of cowbells as they wander around freely. A paradise for walkers, there is a huge variety of flora and fauna to be found, including the increasingly rare Brown Pyrenean bear.

The capital of the region is the university town of **Pau**, known as La Ville Anglaise in the nineteenth century because of the British who visited for the curative effect of its mild climate. It lies an easy driving distance from many attractive small towns and villages. **Salies-de-Béarn** is famous for its thermal waters and known locally as the Venice of Béarn, thanks to its riverfront houses. **Sauveterre-de-Béarn** offers splendid views to the south and a sixteenth-century château. The market town of **Orthez** boasts particularly fine old houses in its rue du Bourg Vieux and rue Moncale. Sleepy **Navarrenx** is a bastide town dating back to the fourteenth century. The town of **Mauléon** is overlooked by a castle described in the fifteenth century as the 'strongest castle in Aquitaine'. Basque culture still flourishes in Mauléon and other towns of the Basque country, with restaurants serving traditional dishes such as fish soup and piperade, and many buildings featuring the Basque symbol of good luck – the sun.

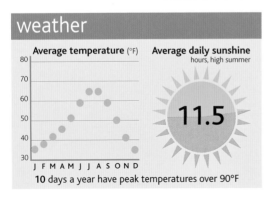

weather

Average temperature (°F)

80
70
60
50
40
30

J F M A M J J A S O N D

Average daily sunshine
hours, high summer

11.5

10 days a year have peak temperatures over 90°F

Property

The coast has always been very expensive, but move inland and prices drop considerably. Estate agents report slow but steady sales to foreign buyers in the past dozen years, and a recent mini-surge thanks partly to the arrival of low-cost airlines.

The central Béarn area, around Navarrenx, is ideal for house-hunting. Close to an excellent road network, it is less than an hour by car to swimming off the sandy coast, skiing in the mountains or a choice of a dozen golf courses. As well as properties that are ready to move into, there is plenty of scope for restoration and renovation. This is not the case slightly further north in Salies-de-Béarn, where a thriving ex-pat community has long since snapped up any restoration projects. This sophisticated little town even has an Irish pub.

Types of property

Architecture in the Pyrénées-Atlantiques falls into three distinct categories according to region. A large eighteenth-century house in the Béarn area in the centre and east is painted in bright colours, has an A-shaped terracotta-tiled roof with a jutting base, and often has a balcony. Smaller two-up, two-down houses are similar in design. Outbuildings such as barns are built of grey cobblestone. Traditional farm and rural houses are usually eighteenth century. They often retain original features such as large fireplaces, bread ovens, carved stone sinks and a 'potager' for keeping soup warm – a stone shelf, set below a window, with a fire beneath it.

The eight-bedroom maison de maitre *restored by Gilly and Pierre de Conti (see page 111)*

Basque country, towards the west and south to the mountains, divides in two. Towards the coast and to the north, large houses consist of a main building joined up with outbuildings to form one big property. They have shallow terracotta-tiled roofs, are half-timbered, and painted white with shutters painted either red or dark green – the Basque national colours.

The south of the Basque country, traditionally a poorer area, looks consequently more sober. Houses are smaller, of grey or white stone with matching shutters, and have steep grey slate roofs as protection against the weather. Outhouses are separate.

What can you get for your money?

These price bands are a guide to the properties you might find.

£23–36,000	studio and small amount of land; ruin and barn needing complete restoration
£36–55,000	basic two-bedroom country house needing some work; two- to three-bedroom town/village house in good condition
£55–90,000	habitable mid-range country house; ski chalet; larger restoration project
£90–130,000	four-bedroom country or townhouse in good condition; modern property in excellent condition; eighteenth-century farm restoration project
£130–200,000	eighteenth-century five-bedroom traditional house with ample land
£200–350,000	large character country/townhouse in good condition with pool and views
£350,000+	coastal properties; rare listed building, e.g. converted mill

Points to consider

Allow an increase in price the closer you get to the coast or motorway. For example, a budget of £70–75,000 might buy a glorified cubby-hole in one of the grander apartment blocks in Biarritz or elsewhere on the coast. On the other hand, it could buy a ski chalet in one of the ski stations in the Pyrenees, a four-bedroom house in need of restoration in a Béarnaise town or a large ready- to-move-into eighteenth-century farm with adjacent barn for conversion into a *gîte*.

Even picturesque hamlets of twenty-five houses or fewer are rarely more than ten minutes away from shops. For example, the small fortified town of Navarrenx itself, with a population of little more than 1,200, boasts post office and banks, two bakers, two butchers, two mini-supermarkets – and six hairdressers.

British families living in the Pyrénées-Atlantiques find it reasonably easy to integrate into their local community, including schools. The school bus picks up pupils from farms, however remote. Life is good.

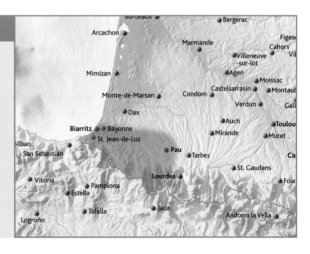

House-hunters

David Exley and Anita Cutts
Budget: £70,000

Having already looked for a second home in western France but without success, conference manager David Exley and computer systems analyst Anita Cutts decided to move their search further south to the Pyrénées-Atlantiques. They had recently renovated their Derbyshire home, and were keen to find a two-bedroom house with either a barn or outbuildings to restore. They hoped to find a traditional house reasonably close to the coast, perhaps with a neighbour to keep an eye on the property when they weren't there.

A nineteenth-century four-bedroom farmhouse in the Haut Béarn with kitchen, bathroom, living room and dining room. Galleried barn for restoration and 1,300 square metres of land. £70,000

Property 1

The first property they saw was in the hamlet of Lube St Christau in the Haut Béarn, part of the Parc National des Pyrénées. Once a working farm, the house had marvellous potential. The small stone-walled kitchen was pretty basic but there was a big dining room and a sitting room with a huge fireplace, flagged floors, dark wood ceiling and a good view of the garden. The pièce de résistance was the huge unused barn ripe for conversion. David and Anita were excited by the setting, and the fact that there was enough work to keep them busy for another ten to fifteen years. 'The barn is the best thing about it. We could put in a second floor and exploit all that space.'

The French tend not to bother with surveyors, but it always advisable to get their advice when buying a property that needs work. In this instance a surveyor pronounced the building structurally sound but pointed out three big jobs that needed doing over the next two years: complete rewiring, replumbing and treating the damp in the walls, at a total estimated cost of £12,000. The advantages

A converted country house in Landes with three bedrooms, open-plan kitchen/living room, one bathroom and an attic. A ruined stable block and 4,000 square metres of land. £84,000

of buying a property for restoration are the fact that the price is open to negotiation and the purchase usually is a safe long-term investment. In this area, there is a high demand for houses like this that have been restored. Judging from other examples, David and Anita were likely to double the value of the house by renovating it.

Property 2

Next it was on to the neighbouring region of Landes, where a fully restored house offered a stunning downstairs space converted from lots of smaller rooms. It had a blue-tiled kitchen area, a large brick fireplace, terracotta floors and exposed beams. The master bedroom was next to the bathroom with a shower and a roll-top bath angled so that the bather could see out of the window. Outside were an attractive garden and courtyard with a hayloft, cow shed and pigsty that could be converted into *gîtes* or additional living space. The main house could be rented for £700 per week to finance the work on the outbuildings. 'It's so inspiring but whatever we did, we would be careful to retain the character of the building.' However, despite being quoted a price of £10–15,000 to re-render and paint the property, they thought it would spoil its character. The only black mark against it was the traffic noise coming from the main road.

A fortified townhouse in Mauléon with six bedrooms, two kitchens, two shower rooms, a dining room and three attic rooms. A courtyard and barn.
£70,000

Property 3

They continued their search in the town of Mauléon in the Basque country. A large six-bedroom townhouse needing a major facelift offered open-plan kitchen and dining room with original oak floors; a main bedroom with original oak panelling and ornate fireplace, with three out of the remaining five secondary bedrooms recently redecorated. The three floors were linked by an impressive spiral staircase. The barn comprised three rooms that needed drastic renovation. Because Mauléon is a heritage site, David and Anita would be eligible for a grant if they wanted to renovate the exterior of the house. The only potential snag was that a dispute over the courtyard had been resolved by a tribunal giving a neighbour rights to keep his chickens there.

Despite feeling that the house was extraordinary value for money, David and Anita decided they didn't want to share their space with the chickens.

Property 4

An eighteenth-century house in Salies-de-Béarn with five bedrooms, an open-plan kitchen/living room and a bathroom. **£55,000**

The last property they saw was in Salies-de-Béarn, a town famous for its thermal waters. This historic house had been converted to have a huge comfortable main living area focused on an open fireplace. The kitchen area had been imaginatively designed with the open work surface placed at an angle to create a traditional triangular kitchen. Upstairs the attic bedroom needed complete renovation. Apart from not having a garden, the other disadvantage was the lack of parking space – a garage nearby would cost about £5,000. David and Anita were advised it was over-priced and that, if they were to offer, they should not pay more than £48,000. However the lack of outdoor space was enough to decide them against offering at all.

Finally they decided to put in an offer for the second house they saw, but eventually the owner decided to sell to a couple from Belgium who were friends of friends. David and Anita were disappointed, but they plan to return to the area and continue their search regardless.

Ex-pat experience

Gilly de Conti
near Mauléon

Gilly de Conti and her son Nicholas

Originally from Hove, Gilly de Conti met her husband Pierre while living in the Dordogne. After marrying in 1978, they bought an 33 hectare vineyard and made a successful business exporting their wine. In 1993 they moved to the Portuguese Algarve to set up a mango and avocado farm and a trekking centre. But they missed France, its changing seasons and greenery, so seven years later they returned. 'We bought an eight-bedroom *maison de maître* that we could restore, although it was in good enough condition to move in to. It's surrounded by 5,000 square metres of garden and beyond that lie fields on all sides and a view of the mountains. We can see snow on the mountains and still have sun in the garden.' (See page 107.)

They now have a business selling and installing swimming pools, and have settled into the area with their three sons aged twenty, sixteen and four. 'It was very easy because the people here are very friendly. It helped that we all speak French and are quite hospitable and socialize a lot. There's always something going on and there are so many *fêtes* that if you go to those, you're in. They last for two to three days and you eat, drink and dance. If you make the effort, you'll be fine.' British home-buyers tend to integrate easily into the area and are often helped by using local workmen – another good way to meet people.

'Don't be in a hurry to buy a property. Find what you want and try to negotiate a lower price.'

The de Contis can buy everything they need locally, although inevitably there is a bigger choice at Pau and Oloron. 'Because there aren't many English living here, you can't get much in the way of English food or newspapers, though the Intermarché will try if you ask.' The de Contis' youngest son goes to the village nursery school where the twenty-five children are divided into three or four classes. Extra-curricular activities include skiing, walking and camping trips as well as visits to the cinema and theatre in Mauléon. When he is ten or eleven, he will go to the college in Mauléon which is much bigger. Meanwhile, their sixteen-year-old is a weekly boarder at the *lycée* in Oloron where he specializes in electronic engineering, catching the public bus to and from home at the weekends. 'The French education system is wonderful. The discipline is also very good and the children learn how to behave well too. They seem to care more about the children, even sending reports back to a previous school so it can follow everyone's progress.'

'Don't bring your car when coming to live here. Registration is costly and the steering wheel is on the wrong side. It's safer and cheaper to buy French.'

For Gilly, the downside of living here is being unable to speak Basque. 'It is spoken a lot although everyone does speak French. I just don't like not being able to communicate. My four-year-old has Basque and English lessons at school already, he's taught me to count up to five.' Otherwise, although it rains a bit, the weather in general is better than in the UK. While she misses Marmite, digestive biscuits and cheesecake, on the plus side: 'The best things are the fact that there is lots of space, little traffic and a healthy way of life. It's a very safe area with the crime rate in Mauléon at virtually zero. We live one hour from the sea and twenty minutes from the ski slopes, so we really do have the best of both worlds.'

Ardèche

Rhône-Alpes, France

Perched on a cliff above the River Ardèche is Balazuc, a medieval stone village classified as one of 'Les Plus Beaux Villages de France'

websites

www.ardeche-guide.com
the official website for the Ardèche tourist board

www.guideweb.com
a general guide to the region

The South of France has become prohibitively expensive for many British home-buyers. However, a short journey north takes the visitor to the unspoilt and largely undiscovered terrain of the Ardèche. One of the eight departments of the Rhône-Alpes region of France, its landscape is wild and dramatic, with the mighty Rhône river providing an 83-mile border on the eastern side of the region. Within easy reach of both the Mediterranean and the ski slopes of the French Alps, it offers the best of both worlds to the more adventurous home-buyer. The rivers cutting through the region provide opportunities for almost every watersport, while hikers, mountain bikers and horse riders can find the same satisfaction exploring the countryside. It is a rugged country of mountains, moors, forests, rivers and lakes, ancient castles and abbeys. Scattered throughout the department are numerous picturesque historic villages – Balazuc, Beauchastel, Labeaume, Saint-Montant and Vinezac among them – and ancient fortified castles such as Château de Crussdel and the Château de Ventadour.

It was this region that saw the country's most determined support of Protestantism during the sixteenth and seventeenth centuries. Later, thanks to its wild landscape, it became a refuge for the Resistance fighters during the Second World War.

The principal product of the Ardèche is its chestnuts. But its vineyards produce a number of internationally renowned wines such as Côtes du Rhone, Viognier and Saint Joseph. Throughout the region festivities take place in the villages, whether celebrating their history, their produce or the arts.

Where to go

The main towns are **Annonay**, **Privas** and **Aubenas**. Annonay in the north-east is the largest town in Ardèche, and hosts an annual hot-air balloon festival celebrating the Montgolfier brothers who were born there. It is situated in the Haut Vivarais, also known as 'the green Ardèche' – so called because it is threaded with fertile valleys, vineyards and orchards. Privas is the capital and administrative centre conveniently located in the middle of the region. It is an historic town famed for its production of marrons glacés. It lies next to the Eyrieux valley, particularly noted for its orchards of peaches and apricots. To the south-west, Aubenas is Ardèche's busy commercial centre and sits on a hill with splendid views of the River Ardèche. Its pedestrianized historic centre has kept its traditional charms, while its castle is still regarded as one of the best examples of architecture in the Ardèche. The town is also the gateway to the Parc Naturel Régional des Monts d'Ardèche that encloses all the chestnut farms in the area.

Other notable towns are **Largentière** and **Tournon-sur-Rhône**. Largentière is south-east of Aubenas and owes its name to the silver mines that were worked in the fifteenth century. The ancient paved city is dominated by the Bishop's Palace, which stands on a rocky spur. Meanwhile, further north, Tournon-sur-Rhône, a town of elegant tree-lined streets, is situated on the banks of the great river against the backdrop of imposing granite hills.

The Ardèche has three spa towns. **Vals-les-Bains** is situated in the Volane valley and boasts 145 therapeutic springs. Although the springs were discovered in the seventeenth century, the town did not fully flower until the nineteenth, a fact reflected in its period architecture and landscaped parks. The other spas are found at **Neyrac-les-Bains** and **St-Laurent-les-Bains**.

The biggest attraction of the Ardèche must be its world-famous gorges that attract thousands of adventure-seeking tourists during the summer. The entrance is marked by the dramatic Pont d'Arc, a 30-metre-high natural limestone arch that spans the river. The river crashes and splashes through spectacular scenery from there to the Rhône. Underground streams, potholes and caves exist all over the region but the most noted are in the south. They include the Aven Marzal and the Aven d'Orgnac, both of which contain memorable stalactite and coloured stone formations. The Chauvet-Pont is the oldest-known decorated cave in the world, where wall-paintings depict lions, bison, woolly rhinos and bears from over 30,000 years ago.

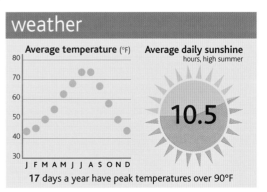

weather

Average temperature (°F)   **Average daily sunshine**
hours, high summer

80
70
60
50
40
30
J F M A M J J A S O N D

10.5

17 days a year have peak temperatures over 90°F

Property

The villages of Antraigues, known for its chestnut markets, is perched high on a forested slope

The Dutch, Belgians and Germans were in the foreign vanguard breathing new life into deserted farms and villages in the Ardèche. The region may be a very small piece of the jigsaw of UK property-buyers in France, but it is well worth finding. With few French inhabitants off the beaten track, and even fewer foreigners, there are cheap properties to be found. British buyers so far tend to be those who do not want British neighbours, and it is not surprising that they home in on a region that is not well represented by British agents. Local estate agencies are getting used to foreign buyers, and bigger ones have at least one excellent English-speaker.

The Ardèche divides north and south, the cut-off point being Privas. But where British incomers once favoured the north, closer to home, these days they gravitate understandably towards the warmer south. Prices in the south can climb to almost double those of its northern half where winters can be bitter. Although prices have picked up considerably – perhaps 25 per cent since the millennium – they are far cheaper than in the neighbouring departments of Drôme to the east and Gard to the south where they can be 20 per cent higher. And far less, of course, than in extortionate British outposts in Provence or the Dordogne.

There are spectacular views in the Ardèche, so expect to pay for them. Prices vary enormously according to location and, obviously, extent of renovation. Today, there are few old buildings crying out for complete renovation although they can be found.

Types of property

Drive fifteen minutes in any direction in the Ardèche and find yourself surrounded by a completely different landscape, with architecture to match. Broadly speaking, houses higher up and in the colder north are more enclosed, made of blacker volcanic stone and with smaller windows. To the south, houses are whitewashed and more open to the warmer weather. A local feature, still evident today, is the heavy stone called *lauze*, used for roofing, that keeps houses warm in winter and cool in summer. An alternative traditional roofing material is *paillisse*, a thatch made from broom held by pine branches.

Because this was once a poor area, many farmhouses began as a small building, often with a communal entrance for people and animals. As owners made their way up in the world, they added extensions and outbuildings. Their legacy is that many larger houses today have the charm of being a collection of smaller buildings that have been linked to make a substantial home.

What can you get for your money?

These price bands are a guide to the properties you might find.

£50–70,000	small one- or two-bedroom country house and garden
£70–100,000	small two-bedroom house, more land and good view
£100–140,000	three-bedroom village house, restored, with terrace
£140–170,000	three-bedroom house, completely restored, ample land
£170–250,000	country stone house, completely restored, pool, lots of ground
£250–650,000	large restored farm buildings, connected, pool, 2–3 hectares

Valvignières has a rich past dating back to Roman times and a reputation for its wine production

Points to consider

The Ardèche remains resolutely traditional, and refuses to have modernity imposed upon it. It is wise to have a smattering of French – whether it is a question of dealing with more important questions at the two main hospitals in the region (Aubenas and Valence) or larger popular markets such as those in Les Vans or Vallon-Pont-d'Arc.

The region is so diverse – and a place to escape to rather than meet up with other British ex-pats – that there is no real focal point for UK incomers. There is a private bi-lingual school (St Régis) in Aubenas – depending on where you live, though, the winding roads may make this an impractical solution in terms of travelling time.

budget flights & transport links

FLY TO NIMES FROM:
London Stansted (Ryanair)

FLY TO LYON FROM:
London Stansted (easyJet)

Ardèche is easily accessible from the A7 Autoroute du Soleil and the TGV fast rail link from Paris, both running alongside the River Rhône which borders the Ardèche for over 75 miles.

The few main roads are good, particularly the N7 that runs alongside the Rhône for the length of the department, but there is no such thing as 'as the crow flies' – secondary roads wind around the hills and mountains, adding enormously to travelling times between a remote village and town.

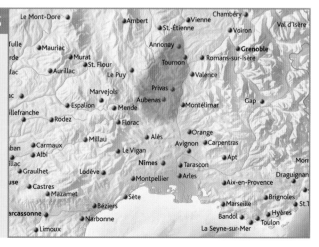

House-hunters

Margaret and John Harpin
Budget: £32,000

Driving through countryside in one of their three Minis is one of the greatest pleasures of engineer John Harpin and his wife Margaret. Where better to pursue their hobby than in the Ardèche, where some of France's most dramatic landscape is to be found? 'We're attracted to the area because we'd like to live within a French community, in true French countryside and enjoy the lifestyle.' Even with the Dales on their doorstep back home, the beauty here staggered them. 'You have no idea what scenery will be round the next corner. Motoring here gives you such an adrenaline rush.' John and Margaret wanted to find a holiday/future retirement home and had a budget of £32,000 to spend.

Property 1

They started their search high up in the mountains where they looked at a remote retreat. Built of grey stone with shutters on the outside, the house was habitable but there was no bathroom. In the kitchen, the original beams were painted orange and the owner's liking for floral wallpaper was evident throughout the house. The master bedroom was quite narrow with a wooden ceiling, and had a fantastic view. Outside, the garage was big enough to hold the couple's fleet of Minis, while the wild garden, complete with orchard and chestnut trees, sloped steeply downwards. 'The house reminds us of a Tardis, small from the outside, but it seems to grow once you go inside and the views are out of this world.' It was evident the house needed some work but as it was below budget there was sufficient finance to allow for the renovations. First on the agenda would be installing a bathroom at a cost of about £1,500 – taking a corner from the ground floor could easily create this. A septic tank was another must and would cost about £2,500. The exterior staircase was picturesque but hardly practical in winter. An internal spiral staircase would resolve the issue.

Overall, though, John and Margaret felt that access to the property was too difficult and likely to seem more so when they got older.

Two-bedroom mountain retreat, with kitchen, living room and cellar. Outside toilet and garage. **£26,000**

Property 2

Next they went to the close-knit community of St-Martin-de-Valamas where a house in the main square was for sale. The main living room was spacious and contemporary. Wooden stairs led up to the first floor, where the master bedroom with a balcony overlooked the square. The bathroom had a white-painted wood ceiling and new fittings, including a shower. Upstairs again led to the second floor, with two further double bedrooms. On the third floor, the attic offered a huge space with a lot of possibility within its exposed stone walls and beamed

Three-bedroom house in St-Martin-de-Valamas, with open-plan kitchen/living/dining area, bathroom, attic, cellar and balcony. Two out of three storeys renovated. Garden.

£34,000

ceiling. Parking availability in the square compensated for the lack of garage space.

John and Margaret loved the location and felt the downstairs two floors of the house were perfect, with potential for the remainder. On Thursday mornings, a market visited the square while the church clock chimed the hours. 'But there's always noise in a community. We don't want to be isolated where we can't hear the world.' The garden, separate from the house, was on two levels including a typical French vegetable plot. The Harpins' only worry was the upkeep of the garden since they would not be there for much of the year. It was reassuring to hear that a retired neighbour already tended it in return for fruit and vegetables and would be happy to continue doing so.

interesting facts

* The Ardèche is 'chestnut' country – 6,000 tons per annum.
* There are over 2,000 potholes and underground caves in the Ardèche.
* The Tanargue massif is the legendary home of the thunder god Taranis.
* 31 per cent of Ardèche is forest land.
* Mount Mezenc is the Ardèche's highest point – 1,700 metres.

Property 3

The third property they saw was on the banks of the Eyrieux River. Half the property was in good order with a large kitchen, a new bathroom, good-sized bedrooms and a huge bright living room with wonderful views of the river. 'The music of the river makes it so peaceful. It's a wonderful setting.' Originally two houses, built in the 1800s, they had been renovated in 1954 when an interconnecting door was added. If the Harpins blocked it off again, they would give themselves extra space for friends or to rent. Conversion above the lounge into bedrooms and an ensuite as well as a further kitchen would cost approximately £3,500. However, the immediate problem

was the damp showing in the upstairs ceiling. The owners insisted that it was just a question of renewing some tiles, a cost of £1,500. Nonetheless, the Harpins were concerned that the water might have damaged the beams, in which case they would be looking at an additional expenditure of £3,000 to put matters right.

Two-bedroom house in the Eyrieux valley, with kitchen, bathroom, living room, attic and three cellars. Garage and terraced garden. **£26,000**

John and Margaret loved the house itself, but felt the size and slope of the garden presented too much of an upkeep problem.

Property 4

Finally, they visited a stone cottage in Lanas. The fourteenth-century living room boasted a number of original features, such as exposed stone walls, small windows, heavy beams and a large fireplace. The bathroom had a typical French shower cubicle but no bath. The wall dividing the bathroom from the bedrooms did not reach the ceiling, thus preventing humidity building up in the enclosed space. Any buyer would need to block the gap and install an electric ventilator. The cellar had a sealed concrete floor ready for conversion – John thought it might make a good workshop. 'Our first impressions, with its archway to the cellar and steps to the front door, was that it was like a medieval castle.'

Pretty two-bedroom stone cottage in Lanas, with kitchen/diner, living room, bathroom and cellar. Completely restored. **£35,000**

As far as John and Margaret were concerned, there was no competition. The townhouse in St-Martin-de-Valamas had everything. They moved quickly, offering the asking price. It was accepted and is now Chez Harpins.

Ex-pat experience

Eileen and Geoffrey Brown
South Ardèche

After eight years renting a house in Provence, Eileen and Geoffrey Brown decided to buy their own home in the Ardèche. Provence was changing, becoming more crowded and more expensive, but the wild and rugged Ardèche offered the attractions of more reasonable property prices, spectacular landscape and prolific wildlife which especially appealed to Eileen. 'I love the environment here. One of my hobbies is photographing the flowers and I enjoy watching out for butterflies, beavers, deer and eagles.' They already knew the area since their daughter had been on a school exchange there and they met the French family who have remained friends to this day.

'Be prepared to be open and friendly and to smile a lot.'

They found an old house on the side of the hill with a terrace overlooking a river valley. It is part of a hamlet of five houses but the local village, with fewer than 3,000 inhabitants, has all the facilities of a small town – doctors, dentists, banks, shops, restaurants and cafés. They were already used to various daily French customs such as putting their rubbish into the communal bin for weekly collection and to greeting friends with kisses. 'We did have some friends here anyway but the local French are very friendly and curious as to why you've come to live here. It's important to be open and friendly back, but you must observe the old-fashioned politenesses of greeting people when you go into a shop and be willing to pass the time of day.'

The local town offers a wide range of activities to join such as martial arts, yoga, choir, keep fit, French for foreigners and so on – all good places to meet new people. 'We are a self-contained and quite solitary couple although I [Eileen] do belong to the local society of carters and carriage drivers who drive horse-drawn vehicles on the annual Route du Châtaigne bringing a token chestnut crop into town. Now we're retired we can enjoy walking our dogs, redecorating the house and the café culture. We swim in the river and I have even canoed and paraglided with my son when he's been to stay.'

'Beware of buying property on land by the river, however picturesque. The storms can be severe and the flash floods devastating.'

Though Geoffrey can get by in French, Eileen speaks it fluently. 'I've even translated for a Dutch lady when the butcher was concerned she was ordering too much meat. When I explained she was feeding forty people for two nights, he was so relieved he has given me the best cuts ever since.'

As anywhere, there are inevitably some snags, such as the low-flying military aircraft, the wild boars that dig up the crocuses, the hot and oppressive sun, the spectacular thunderstorms and the torrential rainstorms. But all that is a small price to pay for the space, the peace and the wildlife untouched by herbicides. 'We have no intention of coming back. We're spoilt here with magnificent scenery, fantastic roads – if you've got a strong stomach – and an extremely good way of life.'

The Andalucían Lakes

T he Andalucían Lakes lie in the Costa del Sol's hinterland among the hills and mountains behind Málaga. Although not officially identified as the Spanish Lake District, it is a useful way of describing the area that encompasses some thirty natural lakes and eighty man-made reservoirs. It is spectacularly beautiful, with dramatic hill and mountain landscapes. The Montes de Málaga, the Sierras de Jobo, Alhama, Tejeda and Almira form the natural borders of the region known as La Axarquía to the east of Málaga. The two largest man-made reservoirs in this area, Lake Iznájar and Lake Viñuela, are only a forty-minute drive from the airport. North of Málaga lie three more vast man-made lakes, created after the damming of the majestic 2,000-foot Guadalhorce Gorge. Not far away is the Laguna de Fuente de Piedra, a natural saline lake that is the only inland breeding ground for flamingos in Europe.

As elsewhere in southern Spain, the history of the region goes back to Palaeolithic times. Remains of Roman occupation have been found, while the

Narrow streets and whitewashed houses characterise the typically Moorish village of Frigiliana

highlights

❊ The Chorro Gorge
❊ Málaga's cathedral
❊ Málaga's English Cemetery
❊ Picasso's birthplace and the Picasso Museum in Málaga
❊ The Moorish citadel of Málaga's Alcazaba

websites

www.spanishforum.org
for advice on building, property and related topics

www.advicecenteronline.
com for the advice centre in Vélez-Málaga offering English-speaking architects, lawyers, accountants etc.
Tel: 09 52 54 90 91

www.surinenglish.com
website of *El Sur* newspaper for Andalucía

Málaga Tourist Office, Pasaje de Chinitas, 4.
Tel: 09 52 21 34 45

Moors left their indelible stamp everywhere – the neatly terraced valleys and irrigation channels, the ruined hill forts, water towers and minarets and of course the celebrated *pueblos blancos* (white villages) that cling to the hillsides among vineyards, olive and almond groves. Since the Christians drove the Moors from Spain, the countryside has remained largely unchanged, with the villagers living off the land largely unaffected by the tourist developments on the coast. The semi-tropical climate has also lent itself to the cultivation of date palms, kiwi fruit, avocados, mangos, citrus fruits and more.

Traditional crafts are found everywhere, whether delicate lace, ceramics, wood carvings, esparto grass baskets, fans and mats and even saddlery. The Moorish culture also lives on in the regional cuisine that depends on local produce, most importantly olive oil and wine. Many of the villages are renowned for their particular specialities and host festivals to celebrate them. Cómpeta is known for its Moscatel grapes and for the bibulous Noche de Vino festival in August. The *ajo blanco* (garlic) is celebrated in Almáchar while Colmenar is famed for its honey and Alcaucín for its cured ham and olive oil.

Where to go

Antequera is a charming market town strategically placed at a crossroads of routes through the region. Prehistoric dolmens or burial chambers have been found on the northern fringes of the town, while twenty-six convents and churches exist within it. Its ruined Alcazaba was the first fortress to be conquered by the Christians in the fight for Granada. The Parque Natural del Torcal is a few miles away, where weird limestone rock formations make one of the most spectacular sights in Andalucía.

To the west of Antequera lies the vast Chorro Gorge, which provides a popular challenge for rock climbers. The nearby town of **Carratraca** is known for its sulphur spa recently reopened, after having had its heyday in the nineteenth century.

The market town of **Vélez-Málaga** is surrounded by strawberry fields, and vineyards producing the Moscatel grape. It is also known for the production of olive oil, sugar cane and ceramics. The town's principal feature is the remains of the Moorish fort on a crag outside town, another bastion in the struggle against the Christian advance. Sixteenth- and seventeenth-century houses are found tucked into the typical Moorish old quarter. There is a weekly Thursday market, and legalized cock-fighting takes place every Sunday. The surrounding white hill-top villages have kept their historic character, thanks to their distance from the tourist beat. **Alcaucín**, **Comares**, **Cómpeta**, **Frigiliana**, **Salares** and **Sedella** are thought to be among the most attractive.

While the attractions of the coast are easily to hand, this part of Spain offers traditional values, a relaxed pace, and plenty of opportunities to explore its history, enjoy its flora and fauna, and to be part of a way of life that has all but vanished in the more popular reaches of southern Spain.

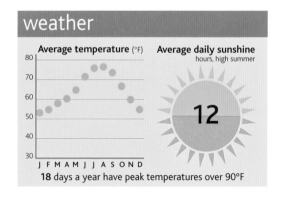

weather

Average temperature (°F)

Average daily sunshine
hours, high summer

12

18 days a year have peak temperatures over 90°F

Property

Two of the largest man-made lakes are magnets for British and other foreign buyers priced out of the Costa del Sol and heading inland in search of bargains. The Embalse (reservoir) de Iznájar has 62 miles of frontage, and the beautiful village of the same name tumbles down to its shores. The other is the smaller Embalse de la Viñuela, to the east and closer to the sea.

Popular with the ex-pat community, Cómpeta is a thriving small town surrounded by vineyards

Some property prices have doubled in as many years. Although traditional architecture is the main attraction, new-build houses are also driving the Viñuela property market as coastal building creeps inexorably inland. As a rule of thumb, the closer to the coast, the more expensive the property. For example, properties round Lake Iznájar are around 20 per cent cheaper.

Types of property

Traditional country houses tend to be small (130 square metres) stone-built, whitewashed farm cottages in a *fanega* (6,000 square metres of land). Downstairs, floors are terracotta tiled, and roofs are made of olive wood beams and local tiles. Ceilings are made of cane, covered in whitewashed daub. It's not unusual to make an attractive feature by exposing and varnishing beams and cane. Upstairs may lead through one bedroom to reach the second, and then again into the third – with no connecting doors.

A larger converted farmhouse might have three bedrooms and several outhouses, one of which probably housed the livestock while another was often the outside kitchen with an open fire and a dome-shaped wood-fired bread oven.

Most old village houses appear small from the outside – but have a lot packed higgledy-piggledy inside. A house may have a bedroom either side of the lounge downstairs and three more tucked away upstairs. Typically, it might have a 'new' bathroom (i.e. possibly twenty years old) and even a spanking new kitchen (ten years old). Expect a patio, and perhaps a sunroof.

However, houses vary in size enormously. Town and village houses can have up to six bedrooms and outbuildings, while some country houses, or *fincas*, may have only a handful of rooms or up to a dozen outbuildings. Mains electricity and water are increasingly available for older buildings. Landline phones are often difficult to connect: satellite phones are a good idea.

interesting facts

❋ At least 5,000 breeding pairs of flamingo populate the Laguna de Fuente de Piedra.

❋ A pan of hot coals underneath the dining table, covered with a thick cloth spread over the family's knees, was the traditional way of keeping warm.

❋ *El Sur* newspaper publishes a weekly English edition, full of property ads.

❋ Rute is a centre for the aniseed liquor industry – the strongest is 55 per cent proof alcohol.

New houses cost approximately £450–£600 per square metre to build. They tend to be one-storey houses in 'traditional' style, with local roof tiles and flooring, pillars, pergola and roof terrace. Most new houses tend to be individual villas rather than whole developments, although a few small new-build clusters are coming on stream.

What can you get for your money?

These price bands are a guide to the properties you might find.

£50–£65,000	country ruin in need of complete renovation/village house needing work
£65–£100,000	plot of building land, 5,000 square metres
£100–£140,000	village house, renovated
£140–£170,000	new villa, with pool and 5,000 square metres of land.

The picturesque Moorish village of Archez is another example of the characteristic layout and architecture of the region.

Points to consider

Vélez-Málaga, just twenty minutes from Viñuela and an hour from Iznájar, has a shopping mall, one of the *El Ingenio* chain, where you can buy everything from up-to-date fashion to the kitchen sink. It also has a cinema, which regularly screens English-language films. There are several golf courses nearby and others are planned.

Many ex-pat kids are happily integrated into local schools, most of which have added Spanish language for foreigners to their syllabus. There is an international school at Rincón de la Victoria.

The municipal pool in Villanueva del Tapia, a neighbouring village to Iznájar, is a popular meeting place for the increasing number of British residents, as are the shores of the lakes which are ideal for swimming and watersports.

budget flights & transport links

FLY TO MÁLAGA FROM:
Dublin (Ryanair)

Manchester, Cardiff and East Midlands (Bmibaby)

London Luton, London Gatwick, London Stansted, East Midlands, Liverpool, Bristol City (easyJet)

London Gatwick, London Luton, Manchester (Monarch)

Southampton (Flybe)

Most of the lakes are ninety minutes' drive away from Málaga or less – Viñuela about forty-five minutes, and Iznájar an hour. Take the N340 from Málaga and the A335 to Viñuela. Other more minor roads also turn off the N340. Roads in the region are good, except for country tracks after heavy rain. There is a network of local buses, but a car is almost essential.

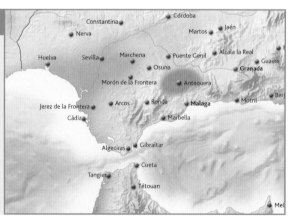

House-hunters

Jean Bentley

Budget: £50,000

Jean Bentley (right) with her friend, Margaret Morse, and Amanda Lamb

Recently married for the second time, support worker Jean Bentley decided to spend her £50,000 savings on a dream home in the sun for herself and her DIY-mad husband John. She chose Spain largely because there were frequent budget flights from nearby Manchester. The Andalucían Lakes appealed because of the countryside's outstanding beauty, its lack of tourist development and the possibility of getting better value for their money inland.

Property 1

*A two-bedroom village house in Periana, with kitchen, bathroom, living room and laundry room. Terrace and outbuildings. **£57,000***

The first port of call was in Periana, a small village famed for its whitewashed streets lined with fragrant orange and lime trees and close to Lake Viñuela. Perhaps it is not surprising that with Málaga airport only forty-five minutes away, 80 per cent of the village population is now British, with property prices rising by 50 per cent in the last two years as a result. Jean felt the village probably offered the best of both worlds and that, living so far from home, it would be reassuring to hear English voices. The two-bedroom village house had lots of character with tiled floors, exposed beams, whitewashed walls and various unexpected nooks and crannies. Jean's first reactions were positive. 'It has a comfortable feel about it. The décor was so easy and cosy. I thought the kitchen was great because of the new units. I've already got all sorts of ideas about lowering floors and other things.'

Outside, there were a number of outbuildings. If she got planning permission, she could convert one into an ensuite bedroom for an estimated £7,000 including labour. If she could persuade her husband John to do the work, she would save a third of the price. The other possibility was to knock down a second outbuilding to enlarge the garden. Doing both would increase the value of the property by £30,000 and put up its potential rental value by £100 per week, from £350 to £450. The house had the potential to be a sound investment, and, although £7,000 above Jean's budget, she could hope to recoup some of the outlay by renting the property in the summer. However, she decided that it just did not feel right for her.

Property 2

*A typical two-bedroom country house in Iznájar, with two reception rooms, kitchen, bathroom and two attic rooms. Courtyard and small plot of land. **£44,500***

Her search then took her to Iznájar, where local people claim the best climate in the area with cool breezes in the summer and shelter from the north winter wind. The property was much bigger than it appeared from the outside. It had few windows but the main living area and both bedrooms had their original beams.

Three-bedroom townhouse in Zuheros, with kitchen, bathroom and living room. Terrace.
£33,000

The kitchen was a good size but needed completely refitting. The most interesting space was the attic, which could be turned into a living area or more bedrooms. Outside there was a patch of land with enough room for a swimming pool. It was quite dark inside but Jean could immediately see the potential. A survey told her that, apart from the house needing a new roof, the upper floor needed strengthening and there was damp on the ground floor – all of which would cost £9,000 to repair. Outside, it was unclear whether or not the vendor owned the land. If she was interested in the property, all Jean had to do to clarify matters was visit the local land registry office and look at the records.

Property 3

Next she travelled further inland to Zuheros, one of the prettiest white villages in the region. It is a largely untapped property market with prices half what they are on the coast. The three-bedroom townhouse had a cool summer room, a kitchen that needed work and a recently completed tiled bathroom. As with many Spanish townhouses, the rooms were rather pokey. 'I liked it and I loved the bright front bedroom. I would knock lots of walls down to make the downstairs open plan.' A local builder quoted £3,000 to install a new kitchen and bathroom. A bigger problem was the damp, a common problem in the old porous walls. The usual solution is to build false interior walls, but they make the room smaller. The price was right for Jean and it would leave enough to do the modernization, but she felt it was too far from Málaga airport to be convenient as a holiday home.

A two-bedroom villa near Cómpeta, with kitchen, bathroom, sun-room, lounge. Terrace, 1,000 square metres of garden and swimming pool.
£79,000

Property 4

Her search ended near the coastal resort of Torrox Costa. A two-bedroom villa outside Cómpeta was over budget but it had a swimming pool and views of the sea. The terracotta-tiled living room 'feels like being at home but with the sunshine'. The kitchen had fitted wooden units, the main bedroom had a comfortable feel, while the pool was 'the icing on the cake' – or at least would be when the pump was replaced. Jean would do well to get a timer switch so the pump could run for two hours a day even when she was back in the UK. The owner had reduced the price by £12,000, having had the villa on the market for seven months. But because there was a road running right behind the property and it was in need of some care and attention, Jean was advised to go in with a lower offer of £74,000. However, although it had everything, she was sufficiently put off by the proximity of the road not to want to take things further.

In the end, she had fallen for the country house by Lake Iznájar. 'There's so much to do, John will think I'm bonkers but he is coming out to see it.' Indeed he did, and eventually they agreed that it was too big a project to take on. They revisited Periana where small developments are going up around the lake and they are hoping to buy there instead.

Ex-pat experience

Clive Jarman
Zuheros

After four years as a walking guide with Andalucían Adventures, Clive Jarman and his wife, Gail, decided to move from Bristol and settle in the village of Zuheros for good. 'We wanted to continue to run walking and painting holidays, and this village offers the ideal combination of the right hotel, the Hotel Zuhayra, and good walking country on the doorstep.'

They already had a happy relationship with the local villagers who think they are slightly eccentric – no Spaniard in their right mind would walk for pleasure over the mountainside. Until recently the Jarmans have been the only foreigners living there, so it has been an 'absolute necessity' to speak Spanish. 'They can understand our English-taught Spanish but it is hard for us to understand the Andalucían dialect in return.' Over the last seven years, they have noticed the increase in tourism. 'We're not overrun by any stretch of the imagination but the Spanish government is providing grants to fund rural tourism and new hotels.' There is a lot of new building in the village but its character remains unchanged. 'Old houses are bulldozed away in a morning. Then new ones are built and painted white, so although they are built from breeze-blocks and not traditional materials, you would never know the difference.' The extent of building is also restricted by the village's situation at the foot of the mountains.

'The Andalucían dialect is very difficult, so you have to work hard to learn the lingo.'

Things have radically improved in Spanish rural life since the demise of Franco in 1975. The village, with a population of only 900, is well serviced by police, bars, school, post office, town hall, library, swimming pool, medical centre, an old folks' home and a seven-day refuse collection that comes every afternoon at 4.30 p.m. 'The road systems in Spain are fantastic now; these, with the high-speed trains and a health system that works, are beginning to make the UK look old hat.'

The village frequently hosts *fiestas* and *romerías* but otherwise Córdoba is only an hour's drive away for theatre and cinemas. As the only English in the village, the Jarmans admit to being occasionally lonely but the UK is just a phone call away and the local bars are friendly. Because of the extremes of temperature in the summer and winter, walking in the Subbética Natural Park is pleasurable only in the spring and autumn, but Clive and Gail are not short of other interests. Within a short time of being there, they bought an interest in a goat farm. The cheese factory in the village takes the milk and distributes the cheese for sale. Clive is also writing a guide book to the region, mapping circular walks that have not been previously recorded, as well as establishing the first estate agency in the village (Tel: 06 69 70 07 63; e-mail: info@alicorsl.com).

'Research the area well before you move, if possible visiting several times over different seasons.'

Giving up life in England has given the Jarmans a tranquillity they did not have before, and a much lower cost of living. Their greatest pleasure is taken in the landscape, walking along goat tracks and old rovers' roads, the ground carpeted in spring flowers and herbs. They have left Bristol a long way behind.

Aveyron

Midi-Pyrénées, France

Spectacularly sited on the River Dourdou, the historic village of Conques is one of the prettiest in the region

One of the most spectacular regions of France is Aveyron, the easternmost department of the Midi-Pyrénées, with its landscape of rushing rivers, dramatic gorges and timeless medieval villages perched high above them. Over the ages, different cultures have left their imprint in the region's many stone monuments, dolmens, menhirs, fortresses, abbeys and churches.

While Aveyron is one of the lesser-known departments of France, its popularity with British second-home-buyers is growing. The region particularly attracts lovers of the outdoor life – stunning scenery and panoramic views make it a magnet for keen walkers and hikers. The rivers provide superb opportunities for canoing, kayaking and rafting and good sport for fishermen too.

Aveyron has a reputation for its cuisine, which includes such treats as *aligot* (a rich mash of potato, butter and Tomme cheese), *tripous* (stuffed sheep's feet in sheep's stomach) and *estofinado* (salt cod cooked in walnut oil). The most famous product of all is Roquefort, the cheese of kings, made from ewe's milk and matured underground in limestone caves above the quiet village of Roquefort-sur-Soulzon. These caves are reputedly the only place to find the particular mould that permeates the cheese to give it its distinctive taste.

Where to go

The capital of the region is **Rodez**, an ancient medieval city on a steep hill dominated by the impressive gothic cathedral of Notre Dame. Although these days the city is perhaps best known as a commercial centre, its ancient skyline altered by modern high-rise developments, it is still possible to wander through numerous original winding streets that conjure up times past. The second principal town is **Millau** in the south, more Mediterranean in feel and spectacularly sited on the River Tarn.

Nine villages in Aveyron have won the coveted title of 'most beautiful French village': Belcastel, Brousse-le-Château, Conques, La Couvertoirade, Estaing, Najac, Saint-Côme-d'Olt, Sainte-Eulalie-d'Olt and Sauveterre-de-Rouergue. All of them are of great historical interest, featuring narrow medieval streets, half-timbered and stone houses, ruined castles and medieval churches – particularly the splendid romanesque example at Conques. One of the villages, **La Couvertoirade**, is among five in the south-eastern corner of Aveyron noted for their connection with the Knights Templar, a military and religious order founded in the twelfth century to protect pilgrims on their way to and from the Holy Land. La Couvertoirade is an enclosed citadel, whose unchanged stone architecture transports the visitor straight back to the Middle Ages. Also noteworthy here are **Sainte-Eulalie-de-Cernon** on the Larzac plateau, which has kept its Templar church, fortified ramparts and towers intact; and **La Cavalerie**, a restored fortified town whose medieval remains can be seen among the fifteenth- to seventeenth-century houses that dominate it.

Sauveterre-de-Rouergue and **Najac** are two of the four 'bastide' (fortified) villages or towns in west Aveyron, built during the thirteenth century. Sauveterre-de-Rouergue is a magnificent example, built round a central square flanked by arcaded medieval houses, while Najac is crowned by a ruined castle on a rocky outcrop. The other two bastides are **Villeneuve-d'Aveyron**, which began as an addition to a monastery but was extended over the years to achieve status as a bastide royale; and **Villefranche-de-Rouergue**, an archetypal bastide village founded in 1252, featuring a regular grid of streets surrounding the focus of an arcaded central square that is home to the weekly market.

The region has a number of ancient châteaux illustrating the area's past military might, including the magnificent Renaissance Château de Bournazel; the Château de Castelnau-Pégayrolles standing proud over the Parc des Grands Causses; the fourteenth-century château at Coupiac; and the Château de Fayet, which was used by Henri IV as a summer residence. There are many more too numerous to mention here.

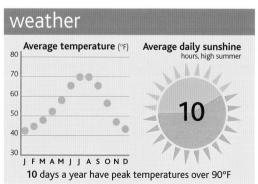

weather

Average temperature (°F) | Average daily sunshine hours, high summer

10

J F M A M J J A S O N D

10 days a year have peak temperatures over 90°F

Property

Large pockets of the Aveyron are truly *la France profonde*. Some farmers still plant seeds, fertilize and harvest according to phases of the moon, and – a fact not entirely unconnected – word-of-mouth is the oxygen of country property sales as much as the small ads in the local newspaper or the occasional free sheet. However fluent your French, you are unlikely to be in the loop, but a good local agent – whether French or one of the few British – will be.

Compared with much of the rest of France, the Aveyron remains relatively cheap even though prices have in general doubled in the last ten years. Obviously, prices have risen more sharply in some property hot spots such as the charming bastide village of Najac and the surrounding area. It is neither too high, nor too wild or remote, with rolling lush countryside that is particularly favoured by the British, while Scandinavians and Germans gravitate towards the south. Apart from Najac, popular areas for British incomers are those around Villefranche-de-Rouergue, Sauveterre-de-Rouergue, the Lot valley (Espalion and Entraygues-sur-Truyère), Conques and

Old stone barns such as this often have fantastic potential for conversion

the gorges of the Tarn river valley. There are also lovely old villages nestling below the vineyard slopes of the Marcillac valley.

Broadly speaking, recent years have seen a slow and steady influx of foreign house-buyers throughout the Aveyron. They are faced with a choice of glorious architecture to suit almost any budget.

interesting facts

❉ Over twenty shops in the village of Laguiole sell its famous eponymous pocket knife.

❉ The signature dish of Michel Bras, whose restaurant displays three Michelin stars, contains thirty young vegetables and herbs from the mountains around Laguiole.

❉ The McDonald's outlet in Millau was trashed by activist José Bové and anti-globalization and anti-fast food protesters in 1999.

❉ Roquefort-sur-Soulzon produces 5 million cheeses annually.

❉ Millau is a leading glove manufacturing town.

Types of property

There are houses with towers like witches' hats, old fortified buildings with roofs made from local heavy *lauze* stone hacked into half-inch thick tiles, little medieval castles with fish-scale *ardoise* slate roofs and sandy-coloured stone houses to match in rustic hamlets. There are occasional half-timbered properties available, while external shutters are to be found everywhere.

Take note that even substantial properties costing well into six figures might have only two or three bedrooms. Château-owners preferred to spend on cavernous reception rooms rather than bedrooms. And always allow for redecoration costs catering for simpler British tastes in place of French elaboration.

A recent Aveyron survey showed 1,670 mills, mainly riverside watermills in the valleys but a few windmills higher up, of which 20 remain working commercial operations. Most of the rest have been converted into residential properties, although a few still wait to be snapped up for restoration.

What can you get for your money?

These price bands are a guide to the properties you might find.

£20–40,000	wrecks and ruins, depending on size, situation and land
£40–50,000	habitable small village house with small garden
£50–70,000	farmhouse to restore
£100,000+	habitable farmhouse, depending on size and land
£400–500,000	top-of-the-range properties

Montredon village in Millau

Points to consider

Remote corners of the department are one of its attractions. The downside is that sparsely populated hamlets and villages cannot support butchers and bakers. Although there are buses and trains, a car is almost essential. Be prepared either to drive for basic supplies, and even further for mini-supermarkets, or learn the ropes of local tradesmen who deliver door to door.

And beware the altitude. A summer purchase is not always what you expect later in the year. Some parts, such as Aubrac in the north-east, are high and cold in winter. Thick walls, with a filling of earth sandwiched between two fat slices of stone, keep farmhouses warm in winter (and cool in summer).

budget flights & transport links

FLY TO RODEZ FROM:
London Stansted (Ryanair)

FLY TO CARCASSONNE FROM:
London Stansted (Ryanair)

FLY TO TOULOUSE FROM:
East Midlands (Bmibaby)

Belfast, Birmingham, Edinburgh, Glasgow, London Heathrow, Southampton (Flybe)

Several trains run daily from Paris, Toulouse, Albi and Montpelier. The A71 motorway runs from Paris to Clermont-Ferrand where the A75 runs to Millau and the N88 to Rodez. The A75 motorway runs from Montpellier. Minor roads are well-maintained though can be hair-raising.

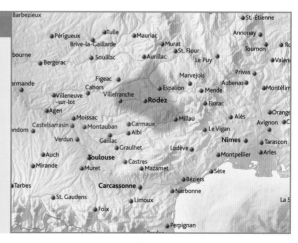

House-hunters

Barry and Liz Crane

Budget: £60,000

Booze cruises were the only thing that had taken Barry and Liz Crane from their home near the Dartford Tunnel to France. Married only six years earlier with seven children between them, they saw France as somewhere 'bigger, prettier and warmer' where they might find a perfect bolt hole away from it all. They were quite open-minded about the sort of property that would make their ideal second home.

One-bedroom cliff-top house in Montjaux, with open-plan living area, kitchen/diner, bathroom, second-floor store-room and large cellar. **£65,000**

Property 1

The first place they visited was the village of Montjaux in the Lévézou, where the houses are squeezed together within the medieval ramparts. The houses tend to have only small gardens, but they do have large cellars traditionally used for storing locally produced wine and walnut oil.

The stone house Barry and Liz viewed was on a cliff with dramatic views over the valley. Once a nunnery, it had been renovated two years earlier and used by its owner as a second home. Although the exterior was a little uncared for, the inside opened up into a spacious living area with a balcony view, and a fitted wooden kitchen. Liz thought it had character, with a great cooker – although it did need more cupboards. The only bedroom was simple and spacious with high ceilings; the second floor was a long space with exposed wooden trusses, used as a store-room – this could be split into two bedrooms. The characteristic large cellar had potential: it could be opened up into a light south-facing room with space for a barbecue outside.

Despite the possibilities, Barry and Liz were disappointed by the lack of outside space so decided they wanted to look elsewhere.

Property 2

Converted barn near Roquefort, with two bedrooms, small kitchen, living/dining room. Large garden. **£40,000**

They travelled to the Grands Causses Nature Park, where a barn near Roquefort had been restored using local stone. The focal point of the property was the living room with its exposed stone walls and massive fireplace. The kitchen had only the basics of a Calor gas hob and water. There was a small shower room downstairs, and wooden steps led up to a spacious bedroom with a wooden floor and ceiling. Outside, a large tiered garden ran down the hill, offering magnificent views of the surrounding countryside. Being so remote, the property did not have a mains water supply. The current owner used a rainwater tank that supplied enough for showering and cooking. However, Barry and Liz could follow the example of many local people and employ a water diviner for £50. If a natural water supply was found, the local authority would fit pipes and a water pump for somewhere between £5,000 and £6,000.

Both Barry and Liz were attracted by the breathtaking setting, but felt the property was too far off the beaten track for them.

Property 3

Next they travelled to the picturesque village of Estaing, where a carefully restored stone house offered a huge beamed living area with an inglenook fireplace and a dining area that would comfortably sit six to ten people. Liz's immediate reaction was positive: 'This is definitely my kind of room.' They particularly liked the tiled floor in the large bright galley kitchen, were impressed by the bathroom that 'had everything', and felt the light and airy master bedroom was 'how a bedroom should be'. Although the garden was big, it had been thoughtfully planted so it could be easily maintained. For Liz and Barry it was: 'Paradise. You can't fault a thing.' The property had already been on the market for nine months and the owner wanted a quick sale, so they were advised to make an opening offer of £75,000.

Stone three-bedroom house in Estaing, with open-plan living/dining room, kitchen and bathroom. Garage and well-maintained garden. **£79,000**

Property 4

Finally they travelled to the north of the region, to the village of Entraygues-sur-Truyère at the junction of the rivers Lot and Truyère. Few foreign house-hunters have discovered the area, so property is particularly good value here. A nineteenth-century cottage in a small village nearby offered lots of period charm, from the rendered exterior with shutters and dormer windows in the traditional shaped roof to the beams and stone fireplace in the living room and the 'warm and intimate' beamed master bedroom. The Cranes liked it. 'It's very quaint and "olde worlde". It reminded us of a dolls' house with its tiny windows but inside it had a surprising amount of space.' All the furniture, apart from a wardrobe in the lounge and kitchen equipment, was included in the asking price. A local antique dealer valued everything between £6,000 and £7,000, with an oak-and-marble dressing table at £1,500. It looked like a very good deal but Barry and Liz felt it was too like a holiday home to fulfil exactly what they wanted.

Traditional nineteenth-century country cottage outside Entraygues, with three bedrooms, living room, kitchen, cellar and attic. Many original features. Pretty garden terrace. **£61,000**

They kept on coming back to the property near Estaing. 'It's everything we're looking for. The owner is in the construction business and has made an excellent job of everything.' They knew they had to move fast but by the time they had got home and were in a position to offer, someone else had beaten them to it. Barry and Liz are not put off. They will be returning to Aveyron to continue their search for their dream home abroad.

Ex-pat experience

Ben and Sammi Pease

Aveyron

Four years ago, UK property prices were beginning to spiral upwards and although furniture maker Ben Pease and his wife Sammi, a sculptress, owned a cottage in Shropshire, his rented workshop was expensive when business was slow. Deciding to cut their losses, they headed as far south in France as they could afford. They specifically wanted to find a property with barns that could be converted into workshops and a *gîte*, 'should all else fail'.

The property they bought consisted of two houses – a derelict farmhouse and a newer one built sixty years ago – plus two big barns, one open-sided barn and six acres of land (ideal for their three Irish setters) and river frontage. 'Although the buildings looked all right, the place was a pigsty. French farmers used to bury things rather than throw them away so we were digging up plastic feedsacks, barbed wire, old shoes, clothes – you name it. It was horrendous.'

For the first few months, their energies were entirely spent restoring the property, eventually moving into the older house so the other could be let. As a result, Ben now works exclusively on other house restorations in the area while Sammi's successful landscaping has also led to commissions.

Their immediate neighbours are mostly farmers. 'They probably think we're dotty. Our property is on a slope so you can see it from miles around, but they come and look round and are all very sweet and flattering. They seem very accepting but we've no idea what they say when we're not there. When we first arrived we met some Brits through the guy who found the property for us and we tended to stick with them because we were desperate for advice. We don't see each other all the time though because we live so far apart.'

'Be prepared to be flexible about the way you earn a living.'

The local villages have small shops that stock all the basics, otherwise Sammi drives to Villefranche where there are a few supermarkets. Although they can get everything they need, she does confess to missing Boots and Marks & Spencer's underwear. 'French underwear is wonderful, but sexy and boned is useless for gardening in.' Otherwise the one thing she can't get used to is the shops shutting for two hours at lunchtime and everything being shut on Sunday so French families can enjoy big lunches and a day devoted to their families.

'The French have a tendency to say "Yes" when they mean "Don't know". Try to clarify whether or not there is a problem.'

'Generally the area is quiet and peaceful and there's no traffic which makes it a real pleasure to drive anywhere. Life is slower, less stressful and there's no sense of having to compete materially with anyone else.' Considering how rural it is and given they pay less than the equivalent in UK council tax, the area is surprisingly well-serviced with fortnightly garbage collections, well-maintained roads and excellent hospitals.

Their gamble has paid off. The Peases feel more comfortable here than they did in the UK and having stuck at it, despite suffering dips in income and having to borrow money, they are now in a position to enjoy their property and use the rent from the second house to pay off the mortgage and make a small profit on top.

How to buy a property in Greece

A general guide

It is essential to employ a lawyer to handle your affairs when buying a property in Greece. There are many English-speaking local lawyers, or you may prefer one based in the UK.

Exchanging contracts

Once your offer has been accepted, a preliminary contract is drawn up in front of the notary. This should contain the names and addresses of the buyer and seller, the description of the property, the price, the means of payment and any other conditions deemed necessary by either party. These may relate to ensuring you obtain vacant possession, that the property is unencumbered by debt, confirmation of the boundaries – or making sure that planning permission has not been granted for a sixteen-storey apartment block right in front of the property.

The Greek inheritance laws, as elsewhere in Europe, may mean that the property is owned by more than one person. Each of them must agree to the sale. If that is the case, it is wise to find out how long it will take to obtain a clear title deed before you sign the contract. A deposit is paid, generally 10 per cent of the purchase, though it may be higher. If the buyer backs out, he will forfeit the deposit. If the seller backs out, the deposit will be returned to the buyer plus an equal sum paid to him by the vendor as indemnity.

The buyer's lawyer is responsible for checking that the title to the property is clear and for carrying out the necessary searches with the land registry. If the property is new or has been extensively restored, he will check planning permission was granted to the builder/developer or previous owner. He will work within the local regulations to ascertain that the 'fixed value' or 'officially estimated price' is usually less than the purchase price. This is important because it determines the purchase tax due plus the notary and lawyer's fees. He will also ensure that the conditional clauses in the contract are ful-filled. Before registering the title deed, make sure you understand the implications as far as inheritance law and tax are concerned. Seek advice from your lawyer.

Completing the contract

When the papers are in order, the final contract is signed before the local notary in the presence of the buyer and seller, their lawyers and, if you do not speak Greek, a translator. At this stage the balance of the purchase price is paid. Greece does not allow 100 per cent ownership, but allows for 'nominees' to hold 1 per cent title to complete the sale.

Additional fees

Expect the purchase tax to be between 9 and 13 per cent of the fixed value, and the lawyer's fee to be between 1.5 and 2 per cent of the fixed value. There is an annual property tax, so you will need a tax number from the local tax office. The tax depends on the location of the property and other variables and is based on tables drawn up by the Greek Ministry of Finance.

Islands

'What shall we tell you? Tales, marvellous tales
Of ships and stars and isles where good men rest.'
James Elroy Flecker, *The Golden Journey to Samarkand*, 1913

Ibiza

Balearic Islands, Spain

The inviting shallow waters of El Torrent lie a short distance south of Sant Josep

Until the 1960s, Ibiza's charms remained unknown to the rest of the world. Since then it has become in turn a hippie hang-out, a magnet for the jet set, a popular package tour destination and a non-stop party paradise. Despite the thousands of tourists who descend on the island during the summer months, Ibiza still has much of its original appeal. There is a wild coastline with beautiful, unspoilt beaches and rocky coves to be found away from the larger resorts. Inland, pine-wooded hills, almond, fig and olive groves, citrus orchards and sleepy traditional villages are dotted across the countryside.

According to recent archaeological evidence, the earliest human settlements on Ibiza were at least 30,000 years ago. Then came the Phoenicians, the

Carthaginians, the Moors and the Catalans from mainland Spain, all of whom left their various marks. Because of marauding pirates, circular watchtowers were built round the coast, some of which remain today.

The island diet is largely based on fish, with specialities including *guisat de peix* (fish stew) and *tonyina al Eivissenca* (tuna, pinenuts, eggs and white wine). Meat dishes include a variety of hearty stews such as *sofrit pagés* (using all kinds of meat). Local wines go hand in hand with *hierbas*, potent herb-based spirits. As elsewhere in Spain, local festivities celebrate village saints' days throughout the year, but in June, bonfires and fireworks all over the island mark the start of summer.

Where to go

Ibiza Town (Eivissa) is the capital, built round the harbour and overlooked by the old town, D'Alt Vila, a warren of narrow streets with ancestral mansions, bars, restaurants and small boutiques. At its summit is the cathedral and castle, while at its foot lies Sa Penya and La Marina, areas full of cafés and shops and, beyond them, the busy harbour. Ibiza new town is modern and not particularly appealing. The town's main beaches are Talamanca to the north and Figueretes to the south.

The major resorts are **Sant Antoni de Portmany** on the west coast, once a tiny fishing village and now a brash package holiday destination; **Portinatx** in the north, a quieter, less overwhelming development; and **Santa Eulària des Riu** in the east. Between them are strung other smaller holiday destinations. **Santa Eulària** is the only one that has clung to real vestiges of its past with its sixteenth-century church and surrounding old town. All resorts benefit from the attractive beaches and rocky coves lapped by translucent aquamarine sea, with plenty of opportunities for watersports, sunbathing or enjoying the beach-side bars and restaurants.

Once off the heavily beaten tourist track, the real Ibiza is still there to be enjoyed. The north of the island has remained the least developed. Tiny hamlets crop up frequently but there are also some quiet picturesque villages with bars and shops used as much by the Spanish locals as the European homeowners. In **Baláfia**, the only place on the island to retain its Moorish name, the houses cluster round two squat towers where, in earlier times, villagers would retreat when invading pirates were on the rampage. **Sant Agnés de Corona** is among the most remote villages on the island despite its proximity to Sant Antoni. **San Llorenç** is a knot of houses grouped round its large church. **Santa Gertrudis de Fruitera** lies at the centre of the island, a popular haunt for ex-pats, with a number of bars and shops. In the south, **Es Cubells** is an attractive cliff-top hamlet not far from Cala Cubells beach and surrounded by various luxurious villa homes.

Among other villages particularly worth visiting are **Santa Inés**, **San Carlos** and **San José** – all of them untouched by major development and surrounded by beautiful Ibizan countryside.

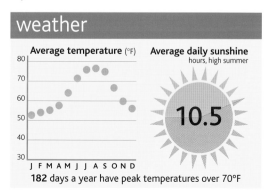

weather

Average temperature (°F)

Average daily sunshine hours, high summer

10.5

J F M A M J J A S O N D

182 days a year have peak temperatures over 70°F

To some extent, Ibiza's old town has managed to keep its historic character with many of the original buildings restored

Property

Despite its reputation as a round-the-clock party island, and three decades of intensive building, Ibiza has plenty to offer the discerning house-hunter. There are still rocky bays that are either empty or have just a few villas. Strict new planning laws intend to keep them that way, forbidding further large-scale developments.

Prices have risen overall by 50 per cent in five years, but remain 25 per cent cheaper than in nearby Mallorca. Industry analysts expect prices in Ibiza to rise steadily by 10 per cent annually over the next few years. The recent hike in prices is partly due to the increase in scheduled flights from the UK to the Balearics, thus making the island more accessible out of season and more attractive to those who want to live there permanently or semi-permanently. The biggest increase in prices is at the bottom end of the market, thanks to those recent changes in planning laws that have put a brake on available property. Prices at the top end of the market – the £1.5 million villa in the middle of the island or the £3 million carbon copy on the coast – have not risen so steeply, and in some cases have dropped in real terms.

Until quite recently, the Germans drove the housing market among foreigners. Now, due to their weak economy at home, they are being forced into retreat. Consequently, some sellers at the more expensive end of the market are willing to negotiate downwards from the asking price, by as much as 10 or 15 per cent. This was unheard of a few years ago when exclusive villas were snapped up within months, if not weeks, of going on sale.

Types of property

Unlike the hinterland of the Spanish *costas*, there are very few, if any, old farmhouses or ruins waiting to be bought for a song and done up. Those old properties that do come up for sale tend to be already renovated and expensive, one of the many dazzling whitewashed houses, cube-shaped and architecturally Moorish-influenced, which are typical of the island. They commonly have thick walls, small windows and an extended porch to give protection from the sun.

What can you get for your money?

These price bands are a guide to the properties you might find.

£90–120,000	one-bedroom apartment
£120–200,000	two-bedroom apartment; or semi-detached two-storey house, communal pool
£200–350,000	two-bedroom detached villa, pool; or three- or four-bedroom penthouse

interesting facts

❖ The Greeks named Ibiza and Formentera the Islas Pitiusas or Pine Islands.

❖ Ibiza has the only river on the Balearic Islands – Río de Santa Eulària.

❖ According to Nostradamus, the sixteenth-century French astrologer, 'Ibiza will be Earth's final refuge' when disaster wipes out the rest of the planet.

❖ Ibiza has its own domesticated dog – *Ca Eivissenc* – thought to have been originally brought to the island by the Phoenicians or the Cathaginians.

| £350–600,000 | renovated three-bedroom farmhouse, pool; or three- or four-bedroom villa, pool; or luxury three- or four-bedroom apartment, overlooking harbour |
| £600,000+ | villa in prime location (sea views) |

The modest resort of Cala Vedella on the south west-coast has a popular sheltered beach

Points to consider

Ibiza, with its excellent infrastructure and communications (broadband everywhere, for example), lends itself perfectly to new media and creative enterprises. Santa Eulària on the east coast is a particular favourite among the British, who, with the Irish, make up about a third of foreign home-buyers. (The Germans make up another third by themselves, with the final third made up largely of French, Italians and Scandinavians.) A sign of Ibiza's increasing popularity among ex-patriates is that the English-speaking international school there, for three- to eighteen-year-olds, is expanding and relocating to a purpose-built facility in the middle of the island.

budget flights & transport links

FLY TO IBIZA FROM:
London Stansted (easyJet)

Scheduled airlines and charter companies fly to Barcelona with connections to Ibiza.

Boats sail from Barcelona, Valencia, Alicante and Dénia.

Fifty years ago, there were a mere dozen cars on the island – now there are more than that number of hire-car companies.

Ibiza's roads are being improved and resurfaced all the time. All corners of the island are accessible by good roads, except for some of the more remote beaches in the north-east. Several bus companies have routes to different parts of the island, with increased services in the summer, including late-night runs.

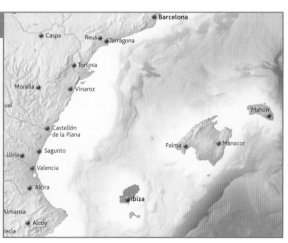

House-hunters

David and Fiona Bolton

Budget: £100,000

Thinking that property in Ibiza would be beyond their budget, carpenter David Bolton and his wife Fiona, a nurse, were pleasantly surprised when they went house hunting. They first came to the island in 1983, fell in love with it and dreamed of buying a two-bedroom property with a garden where Fiona could have her own lemon tree.

Two-bedroom ground-floor apartment in Port des Torrents with two bathrooms, kitchen, open-plan living/dining area. Patio, communal grounds and parking space. **£90,000**

Three-bedroom mountain villa outside Santa Eulària with open-plan living/dining area, kitchen. Two terraces and 1,000 square metres of land. **£108,000**

Property 1

Their search began in Port des Torrents near Cala Bassa beach. The town was developed as a residential area twenty years ago, with all the bars, restaurants and shops laid out in two main streets so the rest of the town remains relatively quiet and traffic-free. There was an apartment for sale in the twelve-unit complex of Los Jardines that offered secluded grounds and a quiet communal pool. The living room was light and bright with a compact, fully fitted kitchen area. A cool breeze blew through the bedrooms, which both contained typically Spanish pine furniture. Air-conditioning for the hottest days, louvred shutters and wrought-iron window grilles made it both cool and secure. David and Fiona were delighted to find somewhere with two bedrooms and bathrooms within their budget. The complex was a pleasant one with eleven English families living there already. An English caretaker would keep an eye on the property when the owners were away. This invaluable service was reflected in the service charge of £915 per year. The Boltons were reassured to hear that the property could be rented out for £350 a week in season.

Property 2

Most of the architecture in the area of Santa Eulària was influenced by Moorish design. On a pine-covered mountain overlooking the town was a white-washed villa with superb views. The villa was tiled throughout in locally made, pale floor tiles. The kitchen had all mod cons. The two terraces had fabulous views across to Santa Eulària. The simple master bedroom had big French windows that opened on to the forest. David thought he might build a wooden deck – no planning permission would be necessary for a structure built of wood. This was a property with style and quality that the Boltons felt had the potential of making a better permanent home than a holiday one. If not regularly

used, there could be a problem of condensation in the winter, but this could be solved by either paying £4,000 for air-conditioning or getting a managing agent to open the windows. The property could have done with a pool but, because the garden was so steep, the landscaping and building would be expensive. They were quoted £18,000 for a 9 x 15 foot pool and told that it would add £30,000 to the value of the property.

Property 3

Ibiza old town is one of the most stylish places on the island to live. It can be noisy, but rental returns are excellent. This first-floor apartment had a large living room with beamed ceiling. Part of it was being used as a dining area. Off it was a small kitchen in need of modernization. The three bedrooms had shuttered windows and original glazed casement doors, while the bathroom had a shower and traditional tiles. The small balcony looked over the busy street. The Boltons quite liked the property, admiring its original woodwork. When considering what to do with the kitchen, they were advised that the window could not be enlarged because it was in a heritage building. Another way of improving things would be to knock down the dividing wall and have one big open-plan living/cooking area at a cost of around £1,500. Neither David nor Fiona were perturbed by the idea of living above a noisy street, and were surprised to hear they could rent the property for £75 a night through the high season.

Three-bedroom first-floor apartment in Ibiza Town with living room, kitchen, bathroom. Small balcony. **£92,000**

Detached, recently renovated two-bedroom holiday house in San José with two bathrooms, living room, dining room, kitchen. Two terraces. **£145,000**

Property 4

Finally they headed for San José, a pleasant resort with many permanent residents. On a hill over-looking the beach is a large four-star hotel. It was built 30 years ago with over 100 luxury villas; although originally part of the hotel, many of these are now privately owned. The one for sale had been recently renovated with marble floor tiles in the living area. The small galley kitchen had everything necessary. A large window let lots of light into the master bedroom, which had plenty of wardrobe space. The guest bedroom would be ideal for their visiting daughter. The renovation was entirely in

tune with the building. The air-conditioning would be perfect for the summer but, for chilly winter nights, there was also underfloor heating. The beach was only a ten-minute walk away, with bars, restaurants and watersports. The possibility of using the hotel's facilities was another advantage.

David and Fiona decided to review the second and fourth properties but in the end decided they were not quite what they were looking for. However, now they know they can afford to live on Ibiza, they are going to spend time looking at more until they find the right one.

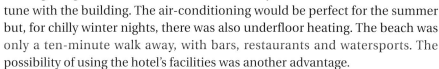

Ex-pat experience

Carol and Michael Winch

Sant Antoni

Owning an apartment in Sant Antoni meant Carol and Michael Winch knew exactly what they were doing when they finally decided to uproot from their Sunderland home and move to the island permanently. Sixteen years earlier they had holidayed with friends in an apartment in The Court, a small 38-apartment complex in Sant Antoni. 'It's a beautiful complex, well-maintained with a swimming pool and gardens. All the apartments are British-owned so there was no language barrier and a really good community atmosphere.'

When one of the apartments came up for sale, the Winches jumped at the opportunity to buy it. Since they owned their own construction business back home, Carol was able to bring their young children Craig and Debbie on holiday in the May and October half-terms and for most of the summer, with Michael joining them whenever work allowed. 'When we weren't there, a residential caretaker kept an eye on the place because we decided we didn't ever want to rent it.'

Things changed on the eve of the millennium when the whole family came over for Christmas and New Year. A bar at the entrance of The Court had been closed for four years. 'We'd grown stale with our business interests at home, so had a family committee meeting and decided to make an offer for it. The Spanish owner had two sons who didn't want to take it over so agreed to sell it to us. The negotiations and purchase were straightforward and then we had to sell our house back home. Our friends thought we were very brave but really the only difficult part was making the decision to do it.'

'Be prepared for the Spanish way of life, which is not the same as at home, even if you are living surrounded by other British people.'

They had never run anything similar – 'But we'd drunk in plenty of bars and restaurants so knew what we wanted.' The first thing they did was demolish the existing bar, rebuilding an English-style country pub with natural finishes, tiled floor and lattice windows brought from the UK. They used Spanish builders overseen by Michael and an architect recommended by the bar's previous owner. 'The Spaniards have a very different attitude to work. They're so laid back, they'll never die of a heart attack. Although we nearly did when it took three months to get electricity in the bar, just in time for the season.' All four Winches found the first year hard going – the work was new to them and they found working in the heat very different from holidaying in it.

'Plan your move well in advance.'

They took Spanish lessons before they moved permanently and last winter continued them in Ibiza. Carol has found learning the language hard. 'I don't have an aptitude for it but as we use Spanish suppliers, I have to be able to order things. Spanish people do use the bar, especially out of season, but all our neighbours are English so I don't use the language enough to learn it properly.'

The friendships they had already established on the island made their move as successful as it has been. Now the bar is up and running, the Winches can relax and enjoy their new-found lifestyle.

Corfu

Ionian Islands, Greece

orfu, the second largest of the Ionian islands that lie off the west coast of Greece, is one of the UK's top ten holiday destinations. It has 135 miles of coastline, varying from long sandy beaches on the west coast to shingly bays on the north-east side of the island, and plentiful rocky coves. With its thousands of cypress trees and olive groves, much of Corfu has more in common with northern Italy than with the Greek mainland or the Mediterranean Greek islands. The highest point of the island is Mount Pandokrátor in the north-east, with spectacular views from its summit. As elsewhere on the island, the mountain provides superb opportunities for walking.

Because of its strategic position in the central Mediterranean, close to both Greece and Italy, the island has been ruled by numerous civilizations, including the Romans, Byzantines, Normans, Venetians, French and, ultimately, the British, who ceded the island to Greece in 1862. Each occupying nation has left

Now a popular island resort, Kalámi was once the home of author Lawrence Durrell

its own mark in the archaeological finds and diverse architectural styles.

The island's cuisine features traditional Greek cooking – *meze* are a familiar starter, consisting of lots of different dishes shared among the diners. Simple dishes use the produce of the island, particularly olive oil, lemons, vegetables and fish. Lamb is the most popular meat, whether in *moussaka* or on skewers. The Italian influence is seen in the pasta dishes, particularly *pastitsio* (layers of pasta and minced meat with béchamel sauce). This can all be washed down with one of the island's local wines such as Santa Domenica, and, of course, retsina. Local festivals and customs abound, such as the unique Easter Saturday ceremony when earthenware pots are hurled from balconies. Otherwise, religious days and saints' days are observed throughout the year.

Where to go

Corfu Town, the capital, has some of the best-preserved Venetian architecture in all the Ionian islands, including the Church of Agios Spyridon which houses the remains of the island's patron saint, Saint Spyridon. Two fortresses flank the picturesque old town, with its cobbled squares and winding alleyways hung about with washing and hiding bars and craft shops. The town boasts the only cricket pitch in Greece, a remnant of British rule. Overlooking it is the Liston, a row of resplendent arcaded buildings modelled on the Rue de Rivoli in Paris, while elegant Italianate buildings complete with balconies and shutters grace other parts of town.

North of Corfu Town is the part of the island most devoted to the package tourist industry, with crowded resorts such as **Kondokali**, **Gouviá**, **Dasia**, **Ipsos** and **Pirgí**. On the north-eastern tip the smaller villages, though popular, have retained their charm and avoided major high-rise development. **Kalámi** is a fishing village, its *tavernas* lining the pebbly beach, with Mount Pantokrátor rising behind it. **Kassiópi** is a picturesque resort centred on a circular harbour, lying between two wooded headlands. Along the north coast the resorts of **Aharavi**, **Róda** and **Sidári** attract many holidaymakers, but only a short way inland are quiet mountain villages in rugged countryside where life goes on pretty much uninterrupted by tourism. On the north-western coast is the breathtaking setting of **Paleokastrítsa**, its three bays gathered round a wooded headland.

The south of the island has less dramatic scenery but is as varied. The freshwater Korissión lagoon was made by the Venetians and is a haven for wildlife, especially wading birds. Unspoilt hill-top villages such as **Vátos**, **Pélekas** and **Sinarádes** all offer an insight into traditional rural life. Narrow streets, whitewashed or painted houses, brilliant flashes of colour from pots of flowers and a tranquil pace of life are only a few miles or less from the packed resorts, picture-postcard fishing villages and stretches of golden sand that fringe the coast.

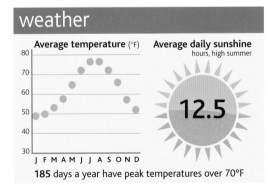

Property

Corfu real-estate analysts estimate property prices on the island have risen by a steady 17 per cent annually since 1999. But, like for like, prices are still a third of those in other prime Mediterranean locations.

The population of Corfu is 110,000, of whom 45,000 live in Corfu Town. About 6,000 of the island's permanent residents are British, most of whom live, or would like to live, in the exclusive twelve-mile stretch of coast and its hinterland between Nissaki and Ag. Stéfanos, in the north-east of the island. Prices here, while still cheap compared to most of Europe, have doubled in four years.

Types of property

The island is rich in desirable properties, from tumbledown village ruins to seaside villas with their own jetties and, thanks to enlightened planning authorities, not a high-rise concrete apartment complex in sight.

A typical Corfiot village consists of houses coloured light ochre, some with outside steps, packed higgledy-piggledy on either side of steep, narrow, winding streets. Walls are thick, windows are small, shutters are dark green, gently sloping roofs are made of straw-coloured Byzantine tiles. Some have narrow balconies, little more than 18 inches wide, with wrought-iron railings painted green, and perhaps a patio. Villas in the countryside share the same characteristics. With one or two storeys, they often have a basement and, of course, more external space: covered verandas, patios, barbecue area, garden and perhaps a swimming pool. Local stone, *siniotiki* – rather like pale sand-coloured Cotswold stone – is used for buildings and terrace walls everywhere.

Bear in mind the value of almost identical houses can vary enormously, by as much as 50 per cent, according to location.

The narrow historic streets of Corfu's old town contain some of the island's most attractive architecture

What can you get for your money?

These price bands are a guide to the properties you might find.

£15–20,000	two-bedroom village ruin, no sea view, far from coast, no mains water, complete renovation required
£20–30,000	as above, but with partial sea view and closer to Corfu Town
£30–40,000	better condition than above, and mains water
£40–50,000	two-bedroom ruin, but good views and near coast
£50–70,000	location and size as above, but in better condition

interesting facts

❋ The Duke of Edinburgh was born in Mon Repos Villa near Corfu Town.

❋ Novelist Lawrence Durrell and his wife, Nancy, lived in Kalami in The White House.

❋ The island of Paxos was once thought to have been cut off from Corfu by a blow from Neptune's trident.

❋ European kumquats are grown uniquely in Corfu.

£70–80,000	one-bedroom apartment in thirty-year-old complex; or well-located inland building plot with sea views
£80–90,000	one-bedroom apartment in Corfu Town, with sea view; or larger one-bedroom apartment in tourist location close to sea; or better building plot, closer to sea
£90–120,000	two-bedroom modern inland property needing lick of paint; or larger building plot close to sea
£120–200,000	good two-bedroom apartment in smart part of Corfu Town; or good modern two-bedroom house on outskirts of Corfu Town and 500 square-metre garden
£200–1,000,000	detached three- to six-bedroom villa, plus pool and garden, in good location
£1,000,000+	special prime location property/estate, e.g. coastal five-bedroom, four-bathroom villa, 4,000 square metres of land and jetty; or inland fourteenth-century Venetian mansion in four hectares

The attractive bay of Koloúra has escaped development

Points to consider

Until recently, it was feasible to buy a building plot, provided the planned architecture fitted in with local Corfiot style and complied with earthquake safety standards. As long as your plot was approximately 4,000 square metres, planning permission was rarely a problem. However, new Greek planning laws are being gradually introduced. In some cases, zoning means reduced availability of building land near the sea. Obtaining planning consent can take time and may be overtaken by new laws forbidding any building on your plot of land. The golden rule is not to buy unless the plot is sold with an existing building permit.

Doing up an old ruin circumvents this problem and is positively encouraged. But remember that transforming a bargain tumbledown goatherd's cottage into the dream Corfiot home may treble your initial outlay and, unlike new buildings, will not qualify for earthquake insurance.

budget flights & transport links

There are **no budget airlines** operating from the UK to Corfu. Explore charter operators via a travel company, through national newspapers or online.

To get to Corfu by car from the UK, drive through Italy to Brindisi, then take a direct ferry. On the island, buses are frequent and cheap but crowded (the summer population rockets from 110,000 to 1.4 million). Taxis are very cheap. A car is a good idea for out-of-town living. There is a good circular main road around the north of the island, and a good main road down to the southern tip, with good minor roads running off them. Most of the island's old dirt roads are now tarmac, albeit with a few dangerous bends. Corfu Town's new one-way system works well, but has not entirely got rid of traffic jams in the summer. Leave your car at the pay park at the old port, and walk.

House-hunters

Johnny and Yvette Rice
Budget: £80,000

Yvette and Johnny have spent a great deal of money over the years on holidays that might or might not have been right for their three children as well as themselves. They felt that, if they bought a holiday home, they could spend at least four to six weeks of the year there, knowing that it would be exactly what they all would enjoy. They had set their hearts on Corfu but initially found that it was difficult to deal with the Corfiot estate agents. 'I think it's a culture clash. In the UK, we're used to wanting everything immediately but things move at a much more leisurely pace here.' They had investigated buying in Spain but that only confirmed that Corfu was definitely the place for them.

Amanda Lamb with D'Arcie and Alberta Rice

Property 1

They began their search in the island's historic capital. There was a four-bedroom apartment in the heart of the old town that had been fully restored. The building itself dated back to 1750, but the open-plan first-floor space had been modernized to contain a long living room, with a wooden ceiling and a fireplace, leading to a fitted pine kitchen. Spiral stairs led up to four bedrooms: a light master bedroom with plenty of built-in storage, and large attic rooms with an additional bathroom that would be ideal for the children. Renovating the exterior of a historic building would need two permits, one from the town hall and another from the archaeological department (the latter costing £700). They would also need a permit if they wanted to install air-conditioning, in which case the unit would have to be positioned out of sight at the back of the house. Johnny and Yvette loved the look and the atmosphere of the place, but felt they needed outdoor space for the children.

Restored four-bedroom apartment in Corfu Town with two bathrooms, kitchen and living room. £84,000

Two-bedroom modern villa near Glyfada beach with bathroom, open-plan kitchen and living room. Covered veranda and garden. £75,000

Property 2

They continued their search at the foot of the Pelekas mountains near the resort of Glyfada. Ten minutes from the beach was a plot where a developer had plans to build two villas. Johnny and Yvette looked at a similar property to give them an idea of what they might get. The open-plan living room was spacious, with a high pine ceiling and air-conditioning for the summer. The kitchen was fully equipped, including modern appliances. The master bedroom also had high ceilings, with French windows leading to a veranda. There was a good-

sized second bedroom and a bathroom with corner bath. The large raised terrace had wrought-iron safety railings. The pool, for which they would have to pay an extra £12,000, was surrounded by walnut, fig and pear trees that are typical of the area. Having a villa built would be cost-effective, but Johnny and Yvette would have to wait twelve months for completion. Both of them loved the situation and the miles of uninterrupted views. They were interested to learn that the owner of the house they saw rented it for £200 per week to friends and family, but could charge £600 if he rented through British newspapers.

Two-bedroom farmhouse with kitchen and living room. Terrace, well, outbuilding and orchard.
£64,000

Property 3

Next they travelled to the north-eastern coast, where they saw a 300-year-old unrenovated farmhouse. It had a big airy kitchen that would need complete modernization, and a living room with a long dining table. The master bedroom was small but had a sensational sea-view. There was also a cool cellar that could be converted into more living space. Although the property had mains water, there was a well on the terrace. 'It is mind-blowing but a big project for us to take on.' They would have to find an architect through recommendation or via the Greek Technical Association, who would redesign it observing the old style and oversee the project. It certainly had the potential to make a great family home and, if they were interested, they were advised to make an opening offer of £55,000.

Property 4

Two-bedroom traditional village house in Kominiata with shower room, kitchen and living room. Shared access to terrace and patio. **£58,000**

Finally they travelled to the south of the island where in the tiny village of Kominiata (population: fifteen) they saw a village house that the owner had renovated over the past four years. There was a bright, light living room with a fireplace for cool winter nights. The bedrooms had attractive wooden floors and were painted in light shades. The large shower room was fully tiled. Outside there was plenty of space, but it was shared with the two neighbouring houses – both of which, however, were up for sale. The middle house was uninhabitable and was on the market for £1,800, while the other was priced at £10,000. So a total outlay of around £70,000 would mean they had control of the patio and a potentially huge property.

Torn between the second and third properties, the Rices returned to the island to have another look, and agreed to buy the off-plan villa with a pool near Glyfada beach. All they have to do now is wait until it is completed.

Ex-pat experience

Anna Asvestas

Kaminaki

In 1976, when she was twenty and single, Anna and three friends backpacked round the Greek islands. 'We went to Corfu simply because the boat took us there and we just stayed here.' Today she and Carole, her friend since primary school, still live there, both married to Greeks and settled into a completely different way of life. 'I had been a secretary in London and just loved the freedom I found here.' She began by working for a car-hire company delivering cars. Two months after arriving she met her husband Asterios, who worked for the same company.

Today they own their own boat-rental business on the north-east coast of Corfu, locally known as 'Kensington-on-Sea', where they rent out small self-drive motor boats and run a water-skiing business. There's no doubt that the island has changed. 'It's become much more built up and more sophisticated since joining the EU. You can buy everything from bananas to English tea bags here now. People originally visited Greece because it was cheap but the euro has definitely meant prices have gone up.' Tourism is a tough business to be in because it is a short season, running from the beginning of May until October: 'We survive, but it's a long time with no business.' During the other six months, Asterios repairs the boats and engines while Anna is kept busy by their children.

'Try to integrate but be sensible, and behave in business as you would in the UK.'

Anna and Asterios have four children: Sophia (seventeen), Dimitri (thirteen), Gabriella (eleven) and Cassandra (eight). All attend or have attended the local school and are bilingual in Greek and English. 'The primary school education is like an English village school where they learn the three Rs, although there is probably more discipline.' The two eldest attend the music high school in Corfu Town, where learning the piano and mandolin is compulsory, although Sophia also plays the clarinet and Dimitri the guitar. 'In Corfu, the grandparents' generation would have finished school at twelve, but now the children strive to go to university. They have a much broader education than they would in England, rather like the French baccalauréat.'

While her children have had to learn English compulsorily since they were nine, Anna has had to pick up Greek over the years. 'It's not easy, because the basics are completely different, but I can get by. Usually I speak in Greek but people reply in English, so their English improves and my Greek doesn't.' Although Anna misses her family, her mother comes out twice a year. Otherwise she feels life is good. 'This is a wonderful life for kids. It's very safe here although the teenagers can get bored. I don't see myself getting old here, but visiting London is a reality check for me. It's dirty, expensive and full of people shopping often in beautiful weather when we would just be on the beach with our friends and their families.'

'Before you move, spend a winter here first and find friends and a job.'

Fuerteventura

Canary Islands, Spain

Fuerteventura's beaches are rated by some to be the best in Europe, ranging from rolling white sand dunes in the north to the flat expanses of sand bordering the Península de Jandía. The island is the quietest, least commercially developed of the Canaries, and the second-largest – though its long narrow shape means that nowhere is more than twenty minutes from the beach. The west coast is more rugged and buffeted by winds off the Atlantic, while the east has calmer shores. Like the other islands in the group, Fuerteventura is of volcanic origin and its landscape is wild and barren, reminiscent of the African Sahara (only sixty-two miles to the east). Lack of rain, volcanic eruptions and Saharan sand blown over the sea saw the end of

Fuerteventura's agriculture. Windmills are dotted across the central plains, where native goats roam wild. The island offers great opportunities for walking and cycling, but is best loved for its watersports and diving sites.

Hundreds of years ago the first settlers on the Canary Islands were known as the Guanches, meaning 'men'. Theirs was a tribal society, and Fuerteventura was split into two fiefdoms that divided the peninsula, Jandía, from the rest, Maxorata. In 1405 the island was taken by the Spanish, who established a base at Betancuria. Gradually Spanish settlers spread across the island while natives went in search of a better life in South America. Over the years the Canaries were constantly under threat from the French, Dutch and British – as well as pirates and slave traders. Eventually, in 1821, all the islands became a province of Spain.

Local culinary delights include fish and shellfish of all kinds. The *mojo* sauce (spicy red chilli pepper) is served with various dishes such as *papas arrugadas* (wrinkly potatoes – small potatoes well salted and cooked in their skins), *pejines* (tiny fish dried and cooked in alcohol), *gofio amasado* (a mix of milk, honey, potatoes, wine and a special flour), and most notably *queso majorero*, cheese from the islands' goats. Every year Corralejo hosts a riotous carnival and all the towns celebrate their saints' days, such as the Día de San Buenaventura (14 July, Betancuria) and de San Sebastián (20 January, La Oliva).

Where to go

The two resorts most popular with the British are **Corralejo** in the north and **Caleta de Fustes** in the east. Corralejo was once a tiny fishing village and, despite development, has held on to some of its original character. What brings people here is the Parque Natural de Corralejo, vast expanses of protected dunes and beach, broken only by the stone windbreaks that protect sunbathers. Caleta de Fustes' low-rise apartments crowd round its horseshoe bay, conveniently close to the airport. **Morro Jable**, in the south, is a quiet fishing village with narrow streets that has been transformed by the addition of hotels, apartments, shops, bars and restaurants, predominantly favoured by the Germans. Other villages, mostly whitewashed buildings with flat roofs basking in the sun, are dotted round the island. Among those particularly worth visiting are **El Cotillo**, **La Oliva**, **Antigua**, **Tefía** and **Ajuy**.

Puerto del Rosario is the island's sprawling capital. Until 1957, it was known as Puerto de las Cabras (port of goats), thanks to the indigenous animals that visited a nearby watering hole. Still a busy working port with a nearby marina and airport, it is home to half the island's inhabitants. **Betancuria** is protected from the winds by its position in a volcanic crater surrounded by the Parque Natural de Betancuria. The road through **Pájara** and **La Pared** leads to **Costa Calma**. Another typically Fuerteventuran town, it lies at one end of the longest, most attractive beach on the island, the Playa de Sotavento.

highlights

✱ A trip to the volcanic island of Isla de los Lobos

✱ An excursion in a glass-bottomed boat

✱ Exploring the dive sites

✱ Sunning yourself on the endless beaches of the Península Jandía or the Parque Natural de Corralejo

websites

www.fuerteventura.com encyclopedic tourist guide to the island

www.fuerteventura.ws the Fuerteventura weather station with links

www.fuerteventura-maps.com small collection of interactive maps

www.fuerteventuragrapevine.com monthly online information magazine including links to estate agents

weather

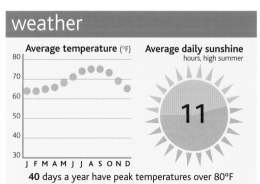

Average temperature (°F)

Average daily sunshine
hours, high summer

11

J F M A M J J A S O N D

40 days a year have peak temperatures over 80°F

Property

Many of the houses in the white village of Betancuría still have their medieval façades intact

Property prices on Fuerteventura have risen by about 20 per cent annually since the turn of the new century, but they remain lower than neighbouring Lanzarote, Gran Canaria and Tenerife – and in general they are also lower than most of mainland Spain. Like the other islands in the group, with their proximity to Africa, Fuerteventura enjoys a year-round, subtropical climate (day-time temperatures rarely dropping below 65°F), so it is not a place that peaks in the summer months and dies in the winter. This makes buying a property there an alluring proposition, whether as an investment or as a second home with a view to permanent residence.

Types of property

The island's planning laws restrict buildings to no more than two storeys (except for a handful of hotels, and even those are only three or four storeys high) – in stark contrast to the popular image of the Canaries being spoilt by patches of high-rise concrete hell. Most properties are link-bungalows in a small complex or resort, or attached houses in chains of half a dozen or so, each with two bedrooms and two bathrooms, car parking, perhaps a sun terrace, and shared facilities such as communal pool and gardens.

Most new properties come with fitted kitchen and bathrooms. What they don't have, because there is no need, is either a fireplace or central heating. Resale properties tend to go on the market with existing furniture.

The dream of doing up a ruined farmhouse or old property remains just that – a dream. Old farmhouses and similar properties that come on the market are almost always renovated and tend to be expensive, at about £200,000. But bear in mind that the top end of the market is still lower than mainland Spain. The most expensive villa – four bedrooms, two bathrooms, plus pool, in 1,350 square metres – is unlikely to cost more than £400,000.

What can you get for your money?

These price bands are a guide to the properties you might find.

£60–85,000	one-bedroom apartment
£85–120,000	two-bedroom apartment; or two-bedroom bungalow
£120–180,000	three-bedroom townhouse/link house
£180–400,000	three-bedroom detached villa, depending on location

A typical white washed house in the hills of Pájara. The parish church in this quiet farming town is one of the island's most historic buildings

Points to consider

Prices, obviously, vary according to location; a prime spot near Caleta harbour and marina, for example, or overlooking a golf course fairway, moves it into the upper brackets. Golf is new to the island. The first golf course, with lakes and streams, in the middle of the island, opened in 2002, with three more planned for elsewhere on the island.

Expenses shared with neighbours in complexes are low. Maintenance costs – for shared gardens, pool, pathways and so on – are about £500 a year, while annual rates are about £200. Add in bills for water and electricity, and annual outgoings total about £1,200 – a fraction of costs you could expect in the UK.

interesting facts

❋ Fuerteventura means 'strong winds'.

❋ Puerto del Rosario is one of the last outposts of the Foreign Legion.

❋ Majorero is the first Spanish cheese to carry the denominación de origén label.

❋ The extreme shortage of rain means the islanders rely on desalinated water or water brought in from the mainland.

budget flights & transport links

There are **no budget airlines** operating from the UK to Fuerteventura. Explore charter operators via a travel company, through national newspapers or online.

The roads on Fuerteventura provide access everywhere on the island, and are excellent, even in the more remote mountain parts of the interior.

Potholes are virtually unknown, and traffic lights do not exist because they are not needed. Traffic is light – a traffic jam consists of two cars in front of you. There is a good bus service (air-conditioned coaches) linking main centres. A car is a good idea, although not essential. Taxis are cheap and car hire costs less than £15 per day.

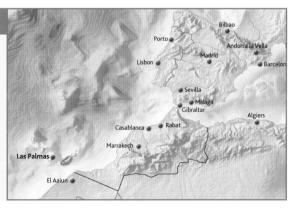

House-hunters

Sandy and Freddy Hooper
Budget: £95,000

When their two daughters left home, Freddy and Sandy Hooper decided the time had come to treat themselves to a holiday home in the sun. They had visited several of the Canary Islands before but felt that Fuerteventura might be the one for them, being less touristy than the others. They wanted to keep their privacy and find somewhere that Freddy could play his music as loud as he wanted.

Two-bedroom, semi-detached villa in Parque Holandés near Corralejo with open-plan living/dining room, kitchen, bathroom. Sun terrace and communal pool. £81,000

Property 1

Parque Holandés is a quiet development just outside Corralejo. An eight-year-old villa offered a spacious open-plan living area that led to the pine fitted kitchen area, complete with table and chairs. It had cream tiled floors throughout and was painted an easy-on-the-eye neutral shade that made the most of the light. The master bedroom benefited from the morning light and the bathroom had two basins and enough room for a washing machine. Outside there was a covered dining area with wide arches giving on to a sunbathing area, while the communal pool was delightfully secluded. Unusually for a building on a complex, there was the possibility of extending it either by filling in the terrace to make an extra room or by adding a third bedroom to the back of the house. As far as the Hoopers were concerned, their outside space was sacred. They were encouraged to hear that the Residents' Association was dividing the communal gardens into private gardens for each property. However, they ultimately felt the property 'just didn't sit right'.

Two-bedroom house in La Pared with living room, kitchen, shower room, solarium. Terrace and garden. £91,000

Property 2

Next, they travelled to the west of the island where they saw a ten-year-old villa in La Pared. The town is small but has two restaurants, two bars and a supermarket that could provide almost everything that Freddy and Sandy would need. The attractive whitewashed house had blue window and door surrounds. Inside, the solarium was light and sunny with white walls and furniture. The spacious living/dining room had a hatch through to the narrow pine fitted kitchen. The bedrooms were a good size and fitted with large built-in wardrobes. Outside the sun terrace looked across the landscape but there was little land attached to the house. An additional potential snag was that the owner had converted the original terrace into the solarium without planning permission. In fact, the council had been informed and said they would not be asking for a fine.

Property 3

They continued their search in Caleta de Fustes. Just outside the busy resort was a brand new complex where they viewed an identical one-storey villa to the one they could buy. Inside, the property had tiled floors throughout. There was a spacious living room with a dining area at one end. French windows led on to a shaded sun terrace. The grey fitted kitchen had ample storage space and work surfaces. The light master bedroom had a fitted wardrobe and a large window. The bathroom was fully fitted and tiled. The disadvantage of this property was that there were neighbours on both sides who might have something to say about Freddy's love of loud music. The important thing to check when buying after looking at a show house is what exactly is included in the asking price. In this instance, the kitchen was not included so another £2,300 would be needed for one the same. Sandy and Freddy's other reservation was that the property would be too exposed to view from passers-by on their way to and from the public toilet and pool.

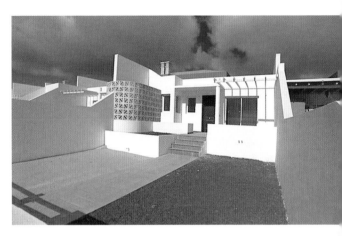

Two-bedroom villa outside Caleta de Fustes with open-plan living/dining room, kitchen, bathroom and utility room. Patio, front and back garden, use of communal pool.
£79,000

Property 4

Finally their search ended in the centre of the island on the fringes of Tuineje. Traditional farmhouses often stay within families for generations so this was a rare find – a house with three ruined cottages. The living area was a blend of traditional and modern with red tiled floors. The bedroom contained a wooden wardrobe and a mezzanine level for storage or, at a push, sleeping. They were shown the layout of one of the ruined houses and were assured that the foundations were sound. Freddy and Sandy thought it was 'interesting'. The problem was knowing where to start. They were quoted another £90,000 to renovate all three cottages at once. It might have been better to make a start by taking the one adjoining the house and converting it into an additional two bedrooms and a bathroom, adding a wall and a gateway round the side of the house where they could build a pool. That would cost around £30,000, with the possibility of an EU grant of £10,000. Although they could see the potential if they wanted to invest that kind of money, they felt it was too ambitious a project.

Nineteenth-century one-bedroom farmhouse on the outskirts of Tuineje with open-plan living room/kitchen and bathroom; three ruined cottages and 2,000 square metres of land. **£95,000**

Having seen four such different properties, Freddy and Sandy thought that the second was the best of the four – although they were concerned there was not enough land. On the other hand, they were quite close to the beach. They returned home to discuss it with their daughters. In the end they decided not to offer, but to continue their search on mainland Spain where they hoped they would find more for their money.

Ex-pat experience

Kenneth and Sallie Wakeham
Corralejo

Bored with their respective jobs in car sales and hairdressing, Kenneth and Sallie Wakeham wanted a change. A holiday in Corralejo gave them the jolt they needed. 'We immediately fell in love with the place. It's the ambience and the fact that it's removed from the hurly-burly you find on the other islands.'

They took Spanish lessons before they moved. 'It seemed common sense and polite. We found it made all the difference. When I meet people here struggling to make themselves understood, I ask them if they have a dictionary. Many of them never even try to learn.'

When they moved, thirteen years ago, Corralejo was just a tiny fishing village. To ensure an income, they bought a studio apartment to rent out and a second apartment for themselves. 'We thought that we'd bask in the sun and drink copious amounts of wine, but we got bored, sold the studio and opened a restaurant. It was what people who came here then wanted – chips with everything. But we were working eighteen hours a day, never saw each other and when we did we rowed. Yes, we were making a profit but that wasn't the point.' Now Sallie does some private hairdressing and has a thriving business selling knickers that she buys wholesale in the UK and sells on a market stall, while Kenneth cooks in a friend's restaurant.

'Come with sufficient funds so that you can return home if it doesn't work out.'

Over the years, living in Corralejo has changed. What was their view to Lanzarote is now a brick wall as they are surrounded by the 'horrifying amount of building'. Kenneth is pragmatic. 'We can't stop it so have to accept it. It seems that everywhere there's an open space, it's built on. I wonder what will happen when all the new people move in. The infrastructure is slowly being created, but will there be enough electricity and desalinated water?'

They have seen several people come to settle here but return home. 'Men can settle on a clothesline. They seem much more adaptable than the women, who miss their home, friends and grandchildren more.' Alcohol is another potential pitfall. 'The English often don't realize the drinks are treble measures here and we have seen them go down that route.' Their friends tend not to be English. They were immediately befriended by the couple who helped them move. 'We didn't have anyone British to play with in those days. The Spanish were very welcoming. Of course now they have benefited from the influx of tourism.'

'Apply English logic when buying property. Rent first if you can and don't leave your brain behind at Gatwick.'

Fuerteventura has entirely fulfilled the Wakehams' expectations. 'The island does engender a lot of feeling. People either love it or hate it. I don't think it's somewhere to come on your own. You need a strong relationship to survive here. All we miss is conversation and the English sense of humour. But the three big pluses here are: safety, freedom and climate. We still love it.'

Estate Agents who helped us

Dialling abroad
If calling from the UK, dial the UK international code first (00), then the country code, then the phone number, omitting the initial zero. The country code for Spain is 34; for France it is 33; for Greece it is 30.

Beaches

The Spanish Algarve
Superior Real Estate Ltd (UK)
Tel: 08700 664660
www.4avilla.com

Isla Canela
Tel: 01206 274195
www.islacanela.co.uk

Elitea Properties (Marbella)
Tel: 09 52 88 44 28
www.eliteamarbella.com

Properties Select (Estepona)
Tel: 09 52 80 86 13
www.propertiesselect.com

Sunshine Estates (Costa de la Luz)
Tel: 09 56 23 90 60
www.sunshineestates.com

Hérault
VEF(UK) Ltd
Tel: 020 7515 8660
www.vefuk.com

Agence Guy (Pézenas)
Tel: 04 67 98 37 77
www.pezenas-immobilier.com

AB Rêves et Soleil (Cap d'Agde)
Tel: 04 67 015 800
www.abreves.com

Océane Immobilière (Cap d'Agde)
Tel: 04 67 00 03 91
www.immostreetpro.com/groupeLMI

Sarl Soph Immobilière (Narbonne)
Tel: 04 68 90 64 65
www.groupe-sm.fr

Orpi-Cabinet Occitan (Pézenas)
Tel: 04 67 98 07 118
www.orpi.com/cabocc

Pézenas Properties
Tel: 04 67 98 53 97
www.pezenasproperties.com

The Campo de Gibraltar
Country Estate Cadiz
Tel: 06 76 98 54 35
www.countryestatecadiz.com

Country Properties (Antequera)
Tel: 09 52 15 12 95
www.cpandalucia.com

Escape2Spain
Tel: 0161 280 7375
www.escape2spain.com

Elitea Properties de San Pedro (Marbella)
Tel: 09 53 88 44 28
www.eliteamarbella.com

Properties Select (Estepona)
Tel: 09 53 80 86 13
www.propertiesselect.com

Campania
Brian A. French and Associates
Tel: 0870 730 1910
www.brianfrench.com

www.tecnocasa.it
Tecnocasa is Italy's biggest online estate agency, region-by-region

www.fiaip.it
A region-by-region directory of estate agents

Murcia
Country Estate Murcia
Tel: 09 68 15 43 81
www.countryestatemurcia.com

Town and Country (Cehegin)
Tel: 09 68 74 28 11
www.tcspain.co.uk

Mercers Ltd (UK)
Tel: 01491 574 807
www.spanishproperty.co.uk

Rent and Sales Costa Cálida
Tel: 06 39 65 32 76

Regency Homes (Torre de la Horadada)
Tel: 06 25 40 15 26
e-mail: torremax@wanadoo.es

Asturias
Inmobiliaria Rivero (Aviles)
Tel: 09 85 56 57 66
www.inmobiliariarivero.com

Inmobiliario Norte Casa (Nava)
Tel: 09 85 71 84 14
www.nortecasa.com

Prada Gestión Inmobiliaria (Cangas de Onís)
Tel: 09 85 84 54 6
www.pradainmobiliaria.com

Gestión Inmobiliaria Maltayo (Villaviciosa)
Tel: 09 85 89 32 16

Reinas Grupo Inmobiliario (Lugones)
Tel: 09 6 31 44
www.reinasgrupo.com

Inmobiliaria Campillo (Llanes)
Tel: 09 85 40 15 82
www.llanesyconcejo.com/campillo

Costa del Azahar
David Headland Associates (UK)
Tel: 01933 353333
www.headlands.co.uk

Parador Properties (UK)
Tel: 01737 770137
www.paradorproperties.com

Oranges and Lemons (Oliva)
Tel: 09 62 85 31 12
www.orangesandlemons.com

La Safor Services (Oliva)
Tel: 09 62 83 90 53
www.lasafor.com

Agencia Libra
Tel: 09 65 57 03 11
e-mail: agencialibra@ctva.es

Inmovidal Inmobiliaria (Pego)
Tel: 09 65 57 03 11
www.inmovidal.com

Countryside

Champagne
Elodie Bruneteaud
24, rue Docteur Lavalle
21000 Dijon – France
Tel: 03 80 38 24 31
e-mail bruneteaud@notaires.fr

Cabinet André Espaullard
Tel: 03 80 91 48 31
Fax: 03 80 91 48 33
www.cabinet-espaullard.fr

Century 21 Lairé Immobilier (Troyes)
Tel: 03 25 71 38 38
www.century21france.fr

La Fôret (Troyes)
Tel: 03 25 43 30 90
www.laforet.com

Guy Hoquet Immobilier (Troyes)
Tel: 03 25 82 16 16
www.guy-hoquet.com

La Rioja
Solozabal
Tel: 09 41 28 70 18
www.solozabal.com

Iregua
Tel: 09 41 24 56 22
www.guia-inmobiliaria.com

Don Piso
Tel: 09 41 25 01 11
www.donpiso.com

ERA Inmobiliaria
Tel: 06 00 37 29 39
www.eraspain.com

Inmobiliaria Cebollos
Tel: 09 41 31 26 76

**CYC4 Inmobiliaria,
Arquitectura y Diseño SL** (Tarazona)
Tel: 09 76 64 12 66

Charente
VEF (UK) Ltd
Tel: 020 7515 8660
www.vefuk.com

North and West France Properties
Tel: 020 8891 1750
www.all-france-properties.com

Tredinnick Immobilier
Tel: 05 45 82 42 93
www.charente-properties.com

Clair-Immo
Tel: 05 45 89 27 75

French Discoveries (Chasseneuil-susr-
Bonnière)
Tel: 05 45 37 69 90
www.french-discoveries.com

Sarl Monnereau Immobilier
(Barbezieux)
Tel: 05 45 78 61 01
www.monnereauimmobilier.com

Cabinet Pellet (Châteauneuf)
Tel: 05 45 66 25 50
www.finepropertyfrance.com

Nowak Immobilier (Civray)
Tel: 05 49 87 03 82
www.nowakimmobilier.fr

Extremadura
Inmobiliaria Induran (Cáceres)
Tel: 00 34 927 53 56 31
www.inmobiliariainduran.com

Rusticas del Noroeste (Salamanca)
Tel: 34 986 731 121
and 34 615 940 002
www.rusticas.com

Country-Estate S.L.
Tel: 34 952 50 62 68
www.countryestatespain.com

Creuse
VEF (UK) Ltd
Tel: 020 7515 8660
www.vefuk.com

Central France Property Search
Tel: 01621 744882
www.cfps23.com

Brunet Immobilier (Guéret)
Tel: 05 55 51 90 90
brunet.immo@wanadoo.fr

Bourganeuf Immobilier (Guéret)
Tel: 05 55 54 95 85
www.limousin-bilingual.com

Century 21 Marcon Immobilier (Guéret)
Tel: 05 55 41 18 38
www.century21france.fr

Agence Immobilière du Centre
(Chateaumeillant)
Tel: 02 48 61 46 39
www.maison.du.centre.free.fr

Mountains

Las Alpujarras
Marjal S.L. (Cádiar)
Tel: 09 58 76 87 43
www.cortijo-andalusi.com

Sunshine Property (Cádiar)
Tel:09 58 85 04 56
www.sunshine-property.com

The French Pyrenees
VEF (UK) Ltd
Tel: 020 7515 8660
www.vefuk.com

Latitudes
Tel: 020 8951 5155
www.latitudes.co.uk

Ardèche
IRS Agence Immobilier (Largentière)
Tel: 04 75 39 27 65
www.irs-immobilier.com

Nogier Immobilier (Aubenas)
Tel:04 75 93 25 60
www.nogierimmobilier.com

Agence Delas (Aubenas)
Tel: 04 75 35 06 76
www.agence-delas.com

Currie French Properties
Tel: 01223 576 084
www.french-property.com/currie

The Andalucían Lakes
Country-Estate S.L. (Málaga)
Tel: 09 52 50 62 68
www.countryestatespain.com

Inmobiliaria La Maroma
Tel: 09 52 51 09 72
www.inmomaroma.com

Inmobiliaria España Autentica
Tel: 09 52 50 30 19
www.espana-autentica.net

Granada Propiedades (Andalucia)
09 58 78 47 51

Aveyron
Sarl Agence Globe Immo
Tel: 05 63 76 48 19
www.tcproperties.com

Select.Properties
Tel: 01296 747045
e-mail: sp@french-houses.demon.co.uk

Action Habitat (Najac)
Tel: 05 65 29 74 74
www.myswfrancehome.com

Islands

Ibiza
Escapes2 Ltd
Tel: 0161 280 7375
www.escapes2.com

Prestige Properties
Tel: 09 71 19 04 55
www.ibizaprestige.com

Vis Ibiza Inmobiliaria
Tel: 09 71 30 07 38
www.vis-ibiza.com

BBS Consulting (San José)
Tel: 09 71 80 07 05
www.bbs-ibiza.com

Corfu
Corfu Property Agency (Corfu)
Tel: 026 61 02 81 41
www.cpacorfu.com

Corfu Real Estate (Aharavi)
Tel: 06 63 06 46 24
www.corfurealestate.com

Niakas Real Estate (Corfu)
Tel: 06 61 03 17 13
www.corfuniakasestate.gr

Fuerteventura
Sunway Fuerteventura (Caleta de Fuste)
Tel: 09 28 16 37 57
www.sunway-fuerteventura.com

Windex Invest SL (Corralejo)
Tel: 09 28 53 50 76
e-mail: match@ctv.es

Fuerhouse Inmobiliaria SL
Tel: 09 28 87 20 83

Aktor Rent
Tel: 09 28 54 90 01
e-mail: info@aktore.de

Plan your house hunting

a checklist for buyers

Professionals you may need
- ☐ Estate agent
- ☐ Solicitor
- ☐ Accountant
- ☐ Surveyor
- ☐ Architect

How to find the right property
- ☐ Which country?
- ☐ Which region?
- ☐ Old or new property?
- ☐ Who will use the property and when?
- ☐ How many bedrooms and bathrooms?
- ☐ What kind of outside space – garden/garage/pool?
- ☐ Ideal climate?
- ☐ Accessibility of local facilities?
- ☐ Accessibility for visitors/tenants?
- ☐ Accessibility to main attractions of region (if letting property)?
- ☐ Will planning permission be readily forthcoming?

How to find properties
- ☐ Local estate agents
- ☐ Local newspapers
- ☐ Internet
- ☐ Foreign property magazines
- ☐ UK foreign property exhibitions
- ☐ UK national newspapers
- ☐ Home-finder agencies

Estate agents
- ☐ Check their qualifications.
- ☐ Be specific about the property you are looking for.
- ☐ Be specific about your budget.
- ☐ Line up a number of properties before you visit.

Before you buy
- ☐ Do not buy without seeing the property yourself.
- ☐ Get to know the region thoroughly.
- ☐ Consider renting in the area before you buy.
- ☐ Visit the property at different times of the day/week/year.
- ☐ Get to know the property market in the area.
- ☐ Talk to locals and ex-pats for advice.

- ☐ Use a surveyor.
- ☐ Be realistic about the amount of work needed.
- ☐ Ask what exactly is included in the asking price.
- ☐ Ask about local planning regulations.
- ☐ Check proximity to mains utilities if unconnected.
- ☐ Check for any rental restrictions attached to the property.
- ☐ Take as much advice as you can.
- ☐ Appoint a solicitor.

If buying off-plan
- ☐ Check plans for future development in the area.
- ☐ Consider how your property will differ from the show property.
- ☐ Find out if there are any restrictions on owners in the community.
- ☐ Find out what the community charge includes.
- ☐ Investigate how much of the infrastructure has been put in place.

Working out your budget
- ☐ Cost of the property.
- ☐ Hidden costs associated with the purchase.
- ☐ Mortgage repayments and set-up costs.
- ☐ Ongoing annual expenses, e.g. utilities, property taxes, rental costs, insurance.
- ☐ Annual cost of upkeep.

If restoring/renovating
- ☐ Professional fees
- ☐ Connection to mains utilities
- ☐ Access

If buying off-plan
- ☐ What is included in the price?
- ☐ Double-check money will be paid in stages.
- ☐ Retain a percentage until six months after completion.
- ☐ What is included in any maintenance charges?
- ☐ Will there be any extra outgoings?

Getting a mortgage
- ☐ Shop around to find which lender is offering the most favourable terms.
- ☐ Take into account the set-up fees.

- [ ] Be prepared to submit detailed accounts of your financial affairs.
- [ ] Decide whether to take out the mortgage in sterling or Euros.
- [ ] If buying a second home abroad, examine the benefits of taking out a home equity loan from your UK mortgage lender.
- [ ] Consider the pros and cons of an offshore mortgage.

Building, restoring, renovating
- [ ] Is planning permission granted for developing the site?
- [ ] How long before it expires?
- [ ] Will it be renewed?
- [ ] Are there other developments in the neighbourhood?
- [ ] Are there ground conditions that may affect the building work, e.g. slope, trees, type of earth?
- [ ] Is there access to mains connections?
- [ ] Check boundaries, rights of way, easements or covenants.
- [ ] Have old property checked over by a surveyor.
- [ ] Will restoration have to conform to any heritage or local council regulations?
- [ ] Are there local planning restrictions?
- [ ] Find an architect through personal recommendation.
- [ ] Be crystal-clear about your expectations.
- [ ] Go through plans with a fine-tooth comb.
- [ ] Appoint a project manager.
- [ ] Are there penalty clauses if work goes over schedule?
- [ ] Keep all receipts to set against rental costs or capital gains tax when the property is sold.

Leaving it all behind
For a permanent move
- [ ] Notify your bank, solicitor, accountant, insurance companies, life assurance companies, hire-purchase companies, credit card companies, rental companies, savings accounts, shopping accounts, companies with whom you have stocks and shares and the Inland Revenue.
- [ ] Inform the Department for Work and Pensions.
- [ ] Cancel any subscriptions.
- [ ] Notify your doctor, dentist, optician and any other practitioners.
- [ ] Cancel relevant insurance policies.
- [ ] Give mains suppliers notice of your move.
- [ ] Send out change of address cards.
- [ ] Settle any outstanding debts.
- [ ] Give reasonable notice to your children's schools and any clubs they may belong to.
- [ ] Cancel milk delivery.
- [ ] Find homes for potted plants.
- [ ] Return library books.

For a temporary move
- [ ] Install/check your burglar alarm.
- [ ] Take out good insurance cover.
- [ ] Leave keys with a neighbour.
- [ ] Cancel all deliveries.
- [ ] Ensure your garden is looked after.

If renting a home
- [ ] Choose a reliable estate agent specializing in property management.
- [ ] Select a tenancy agreement that suits your needs.
- [ ] Clarify who is responsible for maintenance of the property.
- [ ] Compare rentals asked for similar properties before fixing on your own.
- [ ] Ask a solicitor to check the agreement with the letting agent.
- [ ] Include an allocation of responsibilities between the agent, the tenant and yourself.
- [ ] Include restrictions you wish to impose on tenants.
- [ ] Include the conditions for termination of the lease.
- [ ] Check gas and electricity comply with government safety regulations.
- [ ] Check the terms of your insurance policy.
- [ ] Make an inventory (photographic, if necessary).

What can I take with me?
- [ ] Sort out possessions ruthlessly.
- [ ] Make a list of things you want to take.
- [ ] Obtain three estimates from international removal companies.
- [ ] Clarify their conditions of transport.
- [ ] Insure against loss, theft and breakage.
- [ ] Make an inventory of possessions in transit.
- [ ] Give detailed directions.
- [ ] Hire a self-drive van for moving a smaller amount of possessions.

Making yourself at home
- [ ] Notify mains companies of your arrival date (or ask your estate agent to do so).
- [ ] Open a bank account.
- [ ] Register with a local dentist/doctor.
- [ ] Enrol the children in school.
- [ ] Check local requirements for pets (vaccines/tagging, etc.).
- [ ] Try to speak the language.
- [ ] Join in with your local community.
- [ ] Enjoy the local culture and new opportunites.